SECRETS
OF
AMERICA'S TOP
CRAPPIE
GUIDES

SECRETS
OF
AMERICA'S TOP
CRAPPIE
GUIDES

BY
DON WIRTH

PREMIUM PRESS AMERICA
NASHVILLE, TENNESSEE

Secrets of America's Top Crappie Guides by Don Wirth
Published by Premium Press America
Copyright © 2008 by Don Wirth

All rights reserved. No part of this book may be reproduced or transmitted in any form or by any means, electronic or mechanical, including photocopying, recording, or by any information storage and retrieval system, without prior written permission of The Publisher, except where permitted by law.

ISBN 978-1-887654-35-7
Library of Congress Catalog Card Number 2008930732

Premium Press America titles are available at special discounts for use as premiums, sales promotions, fund-raising, and education or for private labeling and licensing. For details contact The Publisher at P.O. Box 159015, Nashville, TN 37215 or call toll free 800.891.7323 or voice 615.256.8484 or fax 615.256.8624.

For additional titles or more information go to www.premiumpressamerica.com

Cover photograph and all interior photography © 2008 by Don Wirth
Cover photo: Tennessee crappie guide Jim Duckworth with two nice Kentucky Lake slabs.
Interior design and cover by BookSetters
Booksetters@aol.com

Printed in the United States of America

1 2 3 4 5 6 / 12 11 10 9 8

INTRODUCTION: CAST OF CHARACTERS

INTRODUCTION: CAST OF CHARACTERS If you're reading this book, you already know that the crappie is an American treasure, a feisty little gamefish that's fun to catch and unrivaled as table fare. But for years I fished for, and wrote about, nothing but bass, and thought of crappie as a no-brainer – just dunk a minnow straight down into a brushpile and reel 'em in, right? Wrong! I quickly discovered that the crappie's frequent mood swings cause it to bite aggressively one minute, then develop a severe case of lockjaw (or pull a disappearing act) the next. Hmmmm, I realized. These fish are every bit as intriguing as bass!

Although millions of people fish for crappie, only a select few are good enough at it to make a living doing it, and these are the experts whose know-how I sought when I began writing about crappie fishing a decade ago. At first I thought they'd be standoffish about revealing their secrets to me (and thus to the masses); on the contrary, they've shared their wisdom with remarkable generosity and the good humor I've come to know as a trademark of those who pursue the elusive papermouth. The result is a different kind of crappie book: it contains tons of hard-core fishcatching insight, but not a single recipe. It's a book for newcomers to the sport as well as those who already know something about crappie fishing, and want to get better at it. I guarantee if you pay close attention to what these guides have to say, you'll consistently catch more and bigger crappie.

Here's some background on the experts you'll find quoted most frequently in this book:

JIM DUCKWORTH, Lebanon, Tennessee, guides for crappie on midstate reservoirs including Center Hill, Priest and Old Hickory. One of the most innovative anglers in the sport, Jim is on the water constantly and has produced a series of excellent videos on crappie fishing. Contact Jim at (615)444-2283 or visit his website, fishingtennessee.com.

GARRY MASON, Springville, Tennessee is a veteran Kentucky Lake guide who has pioneered many productive seasonal crappie approaches. Probably the best artificial lure angler on the crappie scene today, Mason's target-casting tactics will revolutionize the way you fish for crappie. Contact Garry at (731)593-5429.

STEVE McCADAMS, Paris, Tennessee is arguably America's best-known crappie fisherman. A Kentucky Lake guide since he was a teenager, Steve's uncanny ability to find and catch crappie under virtually any condition has made him a living legend. Contact Steve at (731)642-0360 or stevemccadams.com.

HAROLD MORGAN, Madison, Tennessee is one of the most naturally gifted crappie anglers on the planet, a fishermen with a sixth sense for locating and catching crappie in large reservoirs. He guides primarily on Priest Lake but has fished for crappie nationwide. Contact Harold at (615)227-9337.

FRED McCLINTOCK, Celina, Tennessee is a member of the Fresh Water Fishing Hall of Fame. This Pennsylvania native has developed some truly revolutionary tactics for catching crappie from deep, clear lakes with only a minimal amount of cover. Contact Fred at (931)243-2142 or trophyguideservice.com.

Thanks also go to crappie guides Billy Hurt, Spring Creek, Tennessee (901)427-7066 and Tom Moody, Camden, Tennessee (731)593-5429.

Finally I'd like to thank the editors of the publications where much of this material originally appeared: Jason Sowards of *CRAPPIE WORLD*, Doug Stange of *IN-FISHERMAN* and Kurt Beckstrom of *NORTH AMERICAN FISHERMAN*.

—*Don Wirth*
Nashville, Tennessee

Kentucky Lake guide Garry Mason knows that water temperature is the single most important factor influencing crappie mood and location.

CRAPPIE BY THE NUMBERS

Water temperature is arguably the single most important factor determining crappie location, yet I'm amazed at the number of crappie anglers who don't have a temperature monitoring device on board their boats. Today, even the most basic depth finders have surface temperature readout capability; some of these cost only $150 or less including temp probe. And you don't even need a graph to determine water temperature — a simple pool thermometer on a lanyard will work.

I asked Jim Duckworth and Garry Mason how they pinpoint fish throughout the year by monitoring water temperature. I've broken down their advice by 5-degree increments to help get you on fish more quickly throughout the four seasons.

WARM-UP PHASE
35 DEGREES

Crappie location: Crappie will be wintering in the main body of the lake and the deepest tributaries, sometimes at extreme depths. They'll hold tight to the bottom around river and creek channel dropoffs, especially in areas with wood cover in deep water.

Recommended presentations: Vertical jigging with small metal spoons, or tight-lining minnows just above crappie schools, may work, but expect the bite to be very slow.

40 Degrees

Crappie location: Many fish will begin a slow migration into tributary arms as the water temperature creeps upward. An unseasonably warm rain can trigger a mass migration to the mouths of inflowing creeks. Crappie will stack up on opposing points at tributary entrances for a while, then move offshore, where they will suspend around baitfish schools in open water.

Recommended presentations: Electric-troll or wind-drift small twister or tube jigs on long lines through suspending crappie schools. Drift minnows just above suspending fish with heavy sinker rigs.

45 Degrees

Crappie location: Fish will be holding 18 to 30 feet deep on creek channel banks near tributary mouths. Look for crappie staging in brush lining the channel dropoff. In lakes with current flow, fish may move shallower and hold tighter to wood cover in the 12 to 25 foot zone.

Recommended presentations: Bump bottom along the channel dropoff with a minnow rig with a heavy sinker on the bottom. Vertical-jig a small spoon in the same areas; use heavy line and a bronze hook that will straighten under pressure if you hang up in deep water.

50 Degrees

Crappie location: Schools of crappie will begin moving along migration routes leading from creek mouths to spawning areas in the backs of tributaries. Look for scattered groups of fish holding near stumps, brushpiles and stake beds adjacent to the creek channel. Many fish will be in the 15 to 20 foot zone.

Recommended presentations: Continue using the bottom-bumping approach with live bait. Cast small twister jigs to isolated stumps and brush.

55 Degrees

Crappie location: Baitfish become more active and crappie feed more aggressively as they anticipate spawning. Sunshine and mild temperatures mean a gradual warming of gravel/rock banks in tributaries. Many fish will still be in the lower half of the creek arm in 10 to 15 feet of water.

Recommended presentations: Check out rocky areas for staging fish by tight-lining minnows or casting twister jigs.

60 Degrees

Crappie location: Fish will concentrate around wood cover on secondary creek points in the tributaries. Many fish will be halfway back into the creek arm in 8 to 12 feet of water. Check quiet pockets off the main creek channel; these warm quickly and are often full of baitfish.

Recommended presentations: Try dropping tube jigs vertically into wood cover. Cast tube jigs or Slider grubs in sunlit pockets where baitfish are evident.

65 Degrees

Crappie location: Crappie are on the move more than previously as they feed up heavily in preparation for spawning. Fish will scatter in groups along isolated wood cover in the 6 to 10 foot zone, from 1/2 to 2/3 of the way back into the creek arm. Don't overlook shallow water; crappie are aggressive and will chase baitfish into a foot of water now.

Recommended presentation: Cast Slider grubs around wood cover using a fairly fast-moving approach to cover lots of water.

70 Degrees

Crappie location: Males will be moving into shallow spawning areas (4 to 10 feet) in the back half of brushy tributaries. Spawning will take place around crappie attractors including brushpiles and stake beds. Females will be staging near deeper wood cover, waiting for the water to warm before moving shallow.

Recommended presentations: Many males will be in a confined area. Try a minnow fished beneath a float with a split shot placed 2 inches above the hook. Use a cast/retrieve approach with a Slider grub for deeper females.

75 Degrees

Crappie location: Males will be fanning spawning beds in water less than 8 feet deep in murky lakes, up to 12 feet in clear lakes. Females will move in behind them to lay eggs. Spawning takes place in and around brushy cover.

Recommended presentation: Float fishing with live minnows pays off big-time now; huge numbers of crappie will be packed tightly together around prime spawning cover.

80 Degrees

Crappie location: Females will be starting to depart their nests; many will be found on the same deeper wood cover where they staged prior to spawning. Males will be guarding fertilized nests.

Recommended presentations: Nesting males can be caught by casting Slider grubs onto the bed and retrieving them slowly. Females can be taken by casting these same lures to isolated wood cover along tributary migration routes.

85 Degrees

Crappie location: Males will be joining females that are heading back out of the tributaries via the migration routes that brought them into spawning areas earlier. They'll move back toward the main lake via deep channel banks. Many fish will be around major points at the mouth of the creek arm; some will already be in deep water where the creek channel and river channel intersect. Dropoffs are a key structure now; crappie will suspend over the drop around baitfish schools, sometimes 20 to 30 feet deep.

Recommended presentation: Use your electric motor to follow the creek channel out to the main lake, and bump a heavy sinker rig with tube baits and/or live minnows along the bottom.

90 Degrees

Crappie location: Many lakes in the Sun Belt reach temperatures of 90 degrees or more in midsummer. In these waters, the deep pattern rules, with crappie hanging around channel dropoffs lined with standing timber on the main lake and in the deepest tributaries. Here they will suspend for long periods, conserving their metabolic energy to avoid stress. Their depth will be determined in part by the amount of dissolved oxygen in the lake; the fish will be shallower and the bite considerably more active in lakes with noticeable current flow/higher oxygen content.

Recommended presentations: Bump heavy sinker rigs with live minnows along channel drops with minimal wood cover. Jig metal spoons above submerged timber lining channel dropoffs.

Cool-Down Phase

85 Degrees

Crappie location: The lake's temperature will begin gradually dropping with the first cool nights or seasonal rains in early fall. Most crappie will still be relating to deep timber lining river and major creek channels. Fish will be treetop or bottom oriented and may be 25 to 35 feet deep.

Recommended presentations: Vertical fishing with spoons and drifting live minnows on heavy sinker rigs are still the only viable means of reaching these deep fish.

80 Degrees

Crappie location: Some fish inhabiting the main lake will journey to the junctures of river and creek channels, then begin moving into the mouths of the tributaries where they will stack up on channel points, especially those with some wood cover on them. Fish depth may range from 15 to 25 feet depending on water clarity.

Recommended presentations: Spider-rigging live bait on bell sinker rigs directly over schools of deep suspended fish works well now. Long-line electric trolling/drifting with tube jigs pays off in clear lakes.

75 Degrees

Crappie location: Many fish will move into creek arms following schools of small baitfish. Here they will relate to deeper brushpiles lining the submerged channel. The largest concentrations of crappie will usually be found in the first third of the tributary down to 20 feet or so.

Recommended presentations: Brush-probing tactics such as the Kentucky rig (heavy sinker on bottom/minnow and tube jig above) produce well now.

70 Degrees

Crappie location: As baitfish schools progress deeper into the tributary arm, crappie will follow. Most fish will occur halfway up the tributary, where some fairly deep water is still available. Scattered groups of fish will hold around wood cover on flats adjacent to the river channel; 12 to 15 feet is a good depth range to tap now.

Recommended presentation: Casting Slider grubs at scattered wood cover is an effective and fun way to catch crappie now. Because many lakes are extremely clear in fall, back off your target and make extra-long casts with light line.

65 Degrees

Crappie location: Numbers of crappie will begin heading out of tributary arms toward the main lake, migrating via the creek channel. Movement is gradual and will be interrupted by periods where they suspend around brushy cover in the 12 foot zone.

Recommended presentation: Baitfish activity is the key to successful fall fishing, so look for the largest concentrations of bait closest to the creek channel and adjacent structures. Casting grubs continues to be the best overall approach as fish are in scattered groups.

60 Degrees

Crappie location: Large schools of crappie will form on channel bluffs and deep points at or near the mouths of tributaries. Night frosts and cold rains means rapidly cooling water temperatures; fish are likely to be 15 to 20 feet deep as a result.

Recommended presentations: Vertical-fishing with jigging spoons and heavy sinker bait rigs becomes viable now as crappie suspend at deeper depths. Slow-trolling small deep-diving crankbaits can produce surprisingly good catches now.

55 Degrees

Crappie location: The deep point pattern continues to be in effect. Check open water between points for suspending schools of crappie down to around 25 feet.

Recommended presentations: Crankbait trolling will work on schools of fish in the 15-foot zone or shallower. Deeper fish can be taken by vertical fishing with tube jigs or live bait.

50 Degrees

Crappie location: Fish often exhibit a marked movement toward deep water as the lake enters its late fall/winter phase. In some lakes, crappie will be 30 to 40 feet deep, relating to the deepest creek channels and main river channels. Crappie often pack tight to bottom now rather than suspend.

Recommended presentation: Live bait becomes more critical to fishing success in cold water. Use heavy sinker rigs to present small minnows close to bottom.

45 Degrees

Crappie location: Active fish are hard to come by now; most will be glued to the bottom of river and deep tributary channels in the 25 to 40 foot zone. Concentrations of fish will occur near channel bends. Spring holes become crappie hotspots; water temperature may be 10 degrees warmer around springs and fish considerably more active than elsewhere.

Recommended presentation: Bump live minnows just off bottom on heavy sinker rigs, keying on channel bends and spring holes.

40 Degrees

Crappie location: Most fish are on deep channel structure, holding tight to bottom, and will feed only sporadically. Crappies may be 50 feet deep at this time.

Recommended presentation: Super-deep fish are always tough to catch; high winds and frigid weather make scoring even tougher. Live bait lowered to the bottom above a heavy sinker remains your best alternative, but don't get your hopes too high.

35 Degrees

Crappie location: Crappie are nearly dormant as they hug bottom around river and major creek channel dropoffs.

Recommended presentation: Vertical fishing with live bait on heavy sinker rigs.

WHAT TO DO WHEN FISH AREN'T WHERE THEY SHOULD BE

The above water temperature location guidelines aren't hard and fast rules. Crappie have a habit of pulling a disappearing act. If you're on fish one day and can't find them the next, don't panic. Try these strategies instead:

Check open water — When crappie are relating to points and deep channel banks, it's common for them to slide sideways and suspend in open water, especially after a cold front. If you caught fish on points yesterday but can't find them today, idle your boat in a lazy S pattern between two opposing points. Bingo! Usually you can pick up the school suspending in open water. These fish are often catchable by electric-trolling a small crankbait or jig just above the school.

Look shallower — Even on blustery winter days, crappie may slide up from deeper haunts into shallow water to sun themselves and feed. This habit is especially common in midafternoon on calm, sunny days in late winter/early spring, when crappie may creep into water only a foot or two deep. Cast small tube jigs for these fish.

Fish tighter to cover — Crappie, like largemouth bass, relate strongly to wood cover. On days when they're active, they may roam a good distance away from treetops or brush to chase down food. But when they're less active, they stick tighter to cover; presentations that don't knock wood often fail to catch fish. Try lowering a heavy sinker rig with live bait or a tube jig directly into the cover. Once it hits wood, start reeling up slowly and you'll usually score a fish.

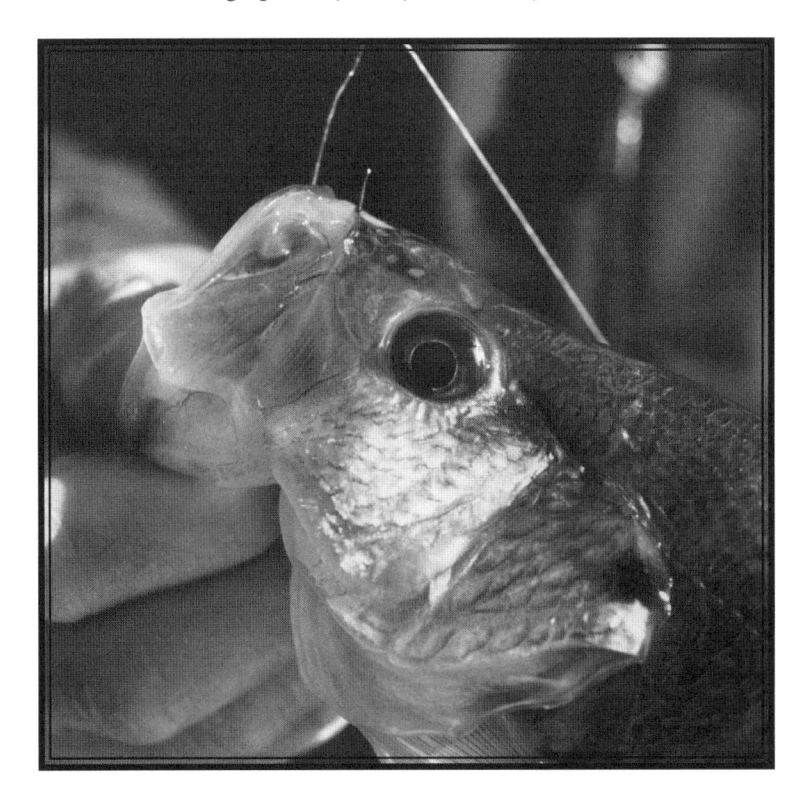

Knowing the best lure or live bait rig to use for the conditions at hand will help you score more strikes. When crappie are suspended in the water column, Dale Hollow Lake guide Fred McClintock relies on the "float 'n fly" – a small jig positioned beneath a bobber.

PROVEN CRAPPIE RIGS

Sometimes it seems as though there are as many different ways to rig a lure or live bait for crappie as there are crappie fishermen. Many rigs work now and then on selected crappie waters, but a select few have stood the test of time and can be counted on to work anywhere crappie swim. Put these "secret weapons" to work on crappie in a lake near you — you'll catch more and bigger fish!

Fred McClintock's Float 'n Fly

Fred McClintock is a master at catching huge smallmouth bass from deep, clear reservoirs. He modified a proven bronzeback system into a killer crappie rig, one that he's used to catch crappie approaching 4 pounds from frigid water.

"The float 'n fly method has steadily increased in popularity over the last decade in Tennessee smallmouth lakes," McClintock said. "Basically the system involves using a long, flexible spinning rod, light line and a 1/16 ounce hair jig. A plastic bobber is attached to the line from around 8 to 12 feet ahead of the lure. Smallmouth bass tend to suspended around rock bluffs and points when the water temperature dips below 50 degrees in late fall/winter. By casting the float/jig combo and letting the jig suspend in the water column for long periods, smallmouths that won't bite an active presentation can be taken."

Crappie, too. When Fred began picking up an occasional slab by this method, he began fine-tuning the rig until he came up with an awesome method for scoring suspending crappie in water all the way down to 38 degrees.

Fred replaces the larger hair jigs used for catching smallmouths with tiny larva-simulating jigs and flies. Once he's located a school of suspending crappie on his graph, he backs off, adjusts the bobber according to the depth of the fish, then casts the float 'n fly to the school. "I want the tiny fly to sink very slowly to just above the level of the school. Once the fly reaches its maximum depth, I'll just let the float sit there, rocking back and forth in choppy water. On calm days, I'll wiggle the tip of the rod slightly to activate the float and the lure beneath it."

The system works best in clear water. On overcast days, McClintock scores most hits on bright-colored flies; on sunny days, white and silver produce better.

Jim Duckworth's Multi-Tube Rig

You can always count on popular Priest Lake (Tenn.) guide Jim Duckworth to come up with an innovative crappie-catcher. He based his Multi-Tube Rig on the rigs river striper fishermen use to catch skipjack herring for bait.

"This rig is especially deadly on crappie that are moving into spawning areas and feeding up heavily in shallow water prior to going on their beds," Duckworth indicated.

Starting with 8 pound mono on a 6-foot medium-action baitcasting rig, the guide ties two 1/16 or 1/8 ounce leadheads rigged with tube jigs to the line with Palomar knots, keeping the jigs 6 inches apart. He leaves extra line hanging off the rear jig and ties a swivel to it another 6 inches below the lure. To this he attaches a 1/8 to 1/4 ounce leadhead rigged with a 3-inch twister grub. Always keep the heaviest jig at the end of the line."

Once Duckworth locates crappie on his graph, he makes a long cast, lets the rig sink to bottom, then reels it slowly and steadily back to the boat. "This setup works on fish hanging tight to bottom as well as suspending crappie. I've had three fish hit on a single retrieve when pulling it back through a school. By varying the weight of the end jig, you can modify the lure for shallow or deep water."

Garry Mason's Carolina Rig

Garry Mason is a master at pulling big stringers of bull crappie from river-run Kentucky Lake. He uses a variation of the bass angler's popular Carolina rig to catch crappie year-round.

"The beauty of the Carolina rig is its ability to present a bait to fish holding tight to bottom structure in a highly natural manner," he pointed out. "I fish this setup on a 6 1/2-foot medium-action baitcasting rod or a stiff 6-foot spinning rod. I like 10 pound mono for my main line and 6 pound mono for my leader."

Garry first passes his main line through a half-ounce egg sinker, then through a red glass bead, before tying a swivel to the tag end.

He then ties a leader between 12 and 16 inches long to the opposite end of the swivel and attaches a #2 gold bait hook to the end. A lively minnow is hooked through the nose.

Mason targets ledges, channel dropoffs and isolated brushpiles with this rig. "I cast it to the shallow side of the structure, let the sinker hit bottom, then move the rod tip sideways in 6-inch increments, pausing to take up slack with the reel between rod sweeps. The minnow is free to swim actively at the end of the leader; when a crappie is in the areas, it goes berserk, which triggers even non-aggressive fish into biting." The guide uses the rig everywhere from shallow tributary ditches to deep channel dropoffs, spring through winter, and occasionally picks up lunker bass and catfish on it, too.

Billy Hurt's Carolina Spider Rig

Billy Hurt uses another style of Carolina rig to probe Kentucky lake's subtle bottom structures. "I combine this rig with multiple 10- and 12-foot crappie poles, the kind that makes your boat look like a giant spider from a distance," he said. "Depending on how many fishermen are aboard, I may run up to 8 poles at once."

Hurt first ties up a good supply of leaders using 18 inches of 6 pound mono with a 1/16 or 1/8 ounce tube jig at the business end, each tied with a Palomar knot. He attaches the tag end of the leader to a swivel, slides a 3/8 to 1/2 ounce egg sinker over his main line, then ties the tag end to the opposite end of the swivel.

With his spider poles held in holders, Hurt adjusts the amount of line out so the jigs barely touch the tops of submerged brushpiles. He maneuvers directly over the cover with his trolling motor. "The secret to tying up this rig properly is to cinch the Palomar knot on the jig down real tight, which causes the hook to ride up at an angle," Hurt said. "This allows you to c-r-a-w-l the jig over brush and tree limbs without constantly hanging up. Of course, hangups will occur occasionally, which is why I keep a bunch of pre-tied leaders on standby."

STEVE MCCADAM'S SLIP-BOBBER TUBE RIG

Most slip-bobber rigs are designed to be fished with live bait. Steve McCadams combines the versatility and precise depth control of a slip bobber with a tube jig in this highly effective rig.

"This slip-bobber rig is designed for casting to fish that are either suspended or holding tight to cover," McCadams explained. Steve uses a 6 1/2 foot medium-action spinning rod with this rig and spools the reel with 6 pound mono. He passes his line through a series of components in the following order: (1) bobber stop, (2) small plastic bead, (3) slip bobber, (4) another small plastic bead. He then ties the tag end to a 1/8 ounce leadhead rigged with a tube. For water deeper than 12 feet or so, he'll pinch a small split shot just above the leadhead.

After determining the depth of the crappie on his graph, McCadams adjusts the bobber stop accordingly, then casts the rig just past his target. "The bobber stop will keep the tube jig at exactly the depth you choose," he indicated. "The best bite always comes when the lure is presented just above the level of the fish or cover." Many fish will hit the jig as it's dropping; others will hit the jig when it's stationary. "Once the jig reaches its maximum depth, avoid moving the rod tip too much," the guide cautioned. "On cold front days, they'll hit it when it's motionless."

RIG IT RIGHT

Many of the rigs featured here can be difficult to tie up on location, especially if (a) your boat is being tossed around in rough water, (b) you're being pelted by rain, or (c) you left your glasses in your truck and can't see clearly enough to pass your line through tiny hook eyes. Here are some tips that'll make preparing these rigs easier.

- Many crappie rigs involve leader lines with a hook or jig on the business end. It's best to trim and rig leaders before heading out for your fishing trip. Store trimmed, rigged leaders in a clear plastic leader tube or a snell keeper.

- Keep components such as swivels, hooks, leadheads, tube lures, etc. in a clear plastic utility box. When you're ready to fish, keep the box on the deck of your boat within easy reach, not buried in a storage locker.

- Keep a jig eye cleaning tool handy. Inevitably the leadhead you pick up will have paint in its eye.

- Crappie can be highly color selective. Soft plastic lures are cheap; buy a large assortment of tube and twister bodies in a full pallet of colors, everything from clear glitter to black, and store them in a compartmentalized utility box. Change colors often until to you determine what the crappie want.

THE ULTIMATE BAIT RIG

Harold Morgan has a reputation for putting his clients on limits of slab crappie all year long. He uses an unusual rig that puts his bait or lure in the strike zone quickly and keeps it there, regardless of depth. Harold calls it the Kentucky rig. "It was developed on Kentucky Lake years ago, before depth finders had been invented," he says. "After the Tennessee River was dammed up and the surrounding countryside was flooded, fishermen used it to locate submerged brushpiles and other crappie-holding structures."

The key component to the Kentucky rig is the heavy sinker tied to the tag end of the line. "The sinker pinpoints dropoffs and cover," Morgan notes. "I use a cylindrical 7/8-ounce bell sinker. It must be heavy enough to keep your line straight down under the boat in wind or current."

Morgan recommends fairly stout tackle with the Kentucky Rig, either a 6 1/2-foot, stiff-action spinning rod, or a medium-action baitcasting outfit. He spools up with abrasion-resistant 8 pound monofiliment line.

Preparing the Rig

Morgan first ties the bell sinker to the end of his line, then sets the rod aside while he prepares two short leader lines. These are cut from a spool of bargain-basement 20- to 30-pound mono. "You want stiff, springy line for your leaders," he insists. (You'll see why in a moment.) Harold trims the leaders to approximately 8 inches, then attaches each to the main line with a loop knot. The bottom leader is tied 18 inches above the sinker; the upper leader 18 inches above the first. This gives your presentation a 3-foot spread, ideal when crappie are suspending.

After the leaders are attached to the main line, Morgan ties a bait hook or lure to their tag ends. " One of the assets of the Kentucky Rig is that you can mix or match your presentation to quickly find what crappie want on any given day," he points out. " If I'm using live bait on one or both of the leaders, I'll attach a light wire crappie hook and bait up with a tuffy minnow. Or I may use 1/32-ounce tube jigs in varying colors — smoke in clear water, chartreuse in murky water, etc. Adjust hook or lure so each leader is 6 inches long, then trim any excess."

Getting Vertical

Morgan fishes the Kentucky rig straight under his boat, using his bow-mounted graph and trolling motor to pinpoint his position over cover and structure. "The depth finder's transducer should be mounted on the trolling motor so it shows exactly what's beneath you," he says. When the boat is over a submerged brushpile, dropoff, logjam or other likely crappie spot, he drops the Kentucky Rig until

THE ULTIMATE BAIT RIG?

the sinker hits bottom, then begins s-l-o-w-l-y reeling it back up. It usually doesn't rise far before a crappie nails it.

Although the Kentucky Rig looks like a tangle waiting to happen, the cheap, heavy monofiliment used for the leaders helps keep snarls to a minimum by keeping your baits or lures at right-angles to the main line.

Crappie often suspend in a tower formation, and reeling the Kentucky rig back up as soon as the sinker taps down is a great way to catch fish that may be anywhere from 1 to 25 feet off bottom. Doubles are very common on this rig, another reason not to use an ultralight rod.

First-timers who use the rig often make the mistake of dragging bottom with the sinker. "In brushy lakes, this will keep you hung up constantly," Morgan warns. "But if a hook gets tangled in brush, don't panic; just tighten down on the reel handle and it'll usually straighten. If the sinker wedges in rocks, jiggling the rod tip gently may dislodge it; if not, break it off and retie."

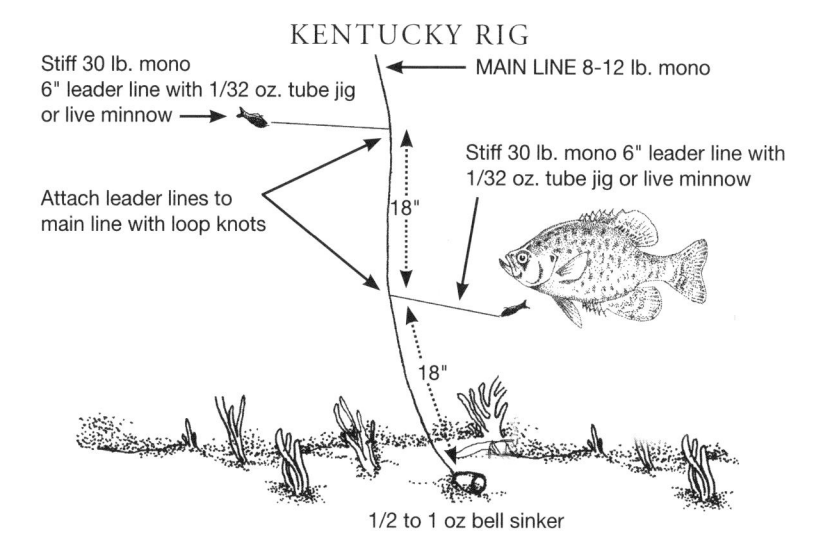

KENTUCKY RIG

Stiff 30 lb. mono 6" leader line with 1/32 oz. tube jig or live minnow

MAIN LINE 8-12 lb. mono

Stiff 30 lb. mono 6" leader line with 1/32 oz. tube jig or live minnow

Attach leader lines to main line with loop knots

18"

18"

1/2 to 1 oz bell sinker

Steve McCadams catches prespawn crappie by targeting their migration routes and staging areas.

STAGING/MIGRATING CRAPPIE

You make your annual spring fishing journey to your usual crappie destination, only to find the lake crowded with fishermen. There are so many boats in the spawning coves, you practically have to take a number to fish a brushpile. Once you do manage to elbow your way through the armada of crappie rigs, you tight-line a stake bed and manage to catch a few scrawny spawners; the net result is barely enough filets for a decent meal.

Are we having fun yet?

All fishermen cringe when they hear the guy at the marina say, "You shoulda been here yesterday!" But in this case, you shoulda been here *three weeks* ago. For that's when the lake's bull crappie were at their biggest — and most catchable.

If you're tired of putting up with big crowds and small crappie during the annual spring bedding season, it's time you took a serious look at prespawn fishing. I have, and it's totally changed my mind about what "prime time" really means as far as our favorite gamefish is concerned.

Steve McCadams knows that prespawn crappie are a different ball game from spawn-time fish. While just about any fisherman armed with a crappie pole and a minnow bucket can catch a fair number of keeper-sized fish during their annual spawning run, McCadams understands it takes an in-depth awareness of the habits of crappie — and a more precise approach — to score big during prespawn.

Moving-Shallow

Do crappie really migrate? "The word *migration* suggests a seasonal long-distance move, such as ducks or monarch butterflies undertake when they fly south for the winter," McCadams said. "Crappie do indeed make seasonal movements, but not over massive distances. They can travel several miles in a big reservoir, but in a small body of water, their movement may be only a few hundred yards. Still, the term is a useful one, because it helps crystallize in the angler's mind the fact that crappie don't sit in one area as the seasons change."

In early spring, crappie are often found holding around deep main-lake structures such as river channel dropoffs and points, McCadams noted. "But as the days get longer and sunlight gradually heats the water into the upper 40- and low 50-degree range, they begin moving toward shallow water. The males are the first to move into the spawning grounds, while the females often wait for conditions to be perfect for egg laying/fertilization; they'll hold in deeper areas adjacent to the beddings grounds, waiting for the air and water temperature to be right and for weather conditions to stabilize."

Most crappie anglers know that peak spawning takes place in 62 to 66 degree water in the backs of creeks and coves, McCadams said. "The biggest problem early-spring fishermen face is determining

STAGING/MIGRATING CRAPPIE

where crappie will be in that elusive 50- to 60-degree range, prior to spawning."

McCadams in convinced crappie use "migration routes" when moving from deep to shallow water during the spring period. He listed the following structures as prime crappie "highways":

- *Creek channels* — "These are the most obvious migration routes in a typical reservoir because they provide a predetermined network of highways from deep to shallow water. The network of tributaries feeding into a main river was there before the reservoir was formed, and crappie instinctively know to use this highway system when transitioning into spawning territory in early spring."

- *Ditches* — "Ditches are considerably narrower and shallower than creek channels and can be either man-made or naturally-occurring. They're typically much harder to locate than creek channels, making them less subject to overfishing. One way to locate 'em is to find a rut in the side of a sloping bank and back your boat out slowly, watching for the ditch to continue underwater on your graph."

- *Points* — "Points serve as a bridge from deep to shallow water, and are easy places for crappie to gravitate to when first moving out of the depths. Crappie will often swim up onto the point, then follow the bank from which the point was formed as it heads back into shallow water."

How deep are migrating crappie? In spring, as a rule of thumb, McCadams expects to find fish along these migration routes anywhere from 12 to 25 feet deep. "Exactly how deep they'll be is dependent on a whole bag of factors, including water temperature and clarity, lake level and weather conditions. They're usually deep when they first start their migration out of open water, then gradually move shallower, but they'll slide back into deep water in cold front conditions."

Points are easy to locate in any body of water, but McCadams is surprised how few anglers fish them in spring. "We've been taught that points are fall structures, which they are, but they're prime places for spring crappie to begin their move into the shallows as well," he noted. Creek channels and ditches, on the other hand, aren't visible to the naked eye; Steve recommends studying a topo map and marking these migration routes with a high-lighter for easy reference. His Ranger boat has graphs mounted at both the console and the bow; the bow unit's transducer is attached to the trolling motor. As he maneuvers his boat directly above the structure, he'll first drop marker buoys along its path to delineate it, then go back and start fishing.

Stop and Go

As crappie move along their migration routes, they may bunch up in large numbers at a certain spot. This behavior, popularly known as "staging," represents a great opportunity for the savvy spring crappie angler. McCadams believes crappie stage for two reasons: "To wait until conditions are just right before moving into their potential bedding areas, and to feed prior to spawning."

Crappie typically stage on points at the mouths of major tributaries, at bends in creek channels and ditches, and near isolated objects such as brushpiles, stake beds, sunken trees and stumps that occur along their migration routes, McCadams indicated. "Staging fish are relatively easy to locate because there's often lots of 'em suspending near the structure or cover. Just look for a cloud of fish or a good grouping of 'hooks' on your graph."

But staging can also occur in a much more amorphous manner, the guide has found. "Often you'll find a huge cloud of crappie suspending in open water in a tributary arm, perhaps 16 feet deep in 30 feet of water. They'll also stage in open water in backwater bays and coves, often around baitfish schools."

Changing lake levels can trigger staging behavior, Steve has found. "Crappie will often suspend in large numbers along migration routes, and in open water, when the lake is rising in spring. Be sure to check for open-water stagers if the lake takes on a sudden rise, as it often does following a couple of days of heavy rain."

McCadams strongly recommends keeping a logbook with maps indicating where, when and under what conditions you catch migrating and staging crappie. "Note the water temperature and clarity, lake level and weather conditions," he suggested. "Often crappie will use the same migration routes and staging areas year after year."

LOADING-THE BOAT

Pre-spawn is a terrific time to catch a boatload of crappie, and arguably the best time of all to bag a trophy slab. "The fish will be bigger, fatter and more concentrated now than at any time of the year," McCadams insisted. Here are some methods the guide employs to catch them:

Multi-pole presentations are a good bet this time of year. "Rig some poles with tiny tube or twister jigs in varying colors, others with live minnows," Steve suggested. "Set your offerings at various depths — some fish will be holding near the bottom, others suspending. Using multiple poles is a good way to fish a large migration route such as a creek channel because it enables you to cut a wide swath while moving along the 'highway'."

Bobber rigs are also useful, for they offer exact depth regulation when presenting live bait to suspending fish or crappie holding near objects. "Many anglers have never fished a jig on a bobber; this works great in cold water in early spring, for it suspends the jig at the exact level of the fish." McCadams especially likes the bobber/jig combo in choppy water because "the waves do the jigging for you."

Bottom-bumping rigs like the Kentucky rig are the most cover-intensive method McCadams uses in early spring. "Move along migration routes and lower the sinker until it contacts bottom or cover, then s-l-o-w-l-y reel upward. The leader hooks can be rigged with minnows, tube jigs or a combination of both. Expect two fish at once when you get into a school — the lower hook will catch crappie holding tight to bottom, while the upper hook will catch fish suspending above the cover."

Trolling crankbaits is an awesomely effective way to catch staging fish suspending in open water. "On some days they'll hit a big deep-diving bass plug, but for consistent results, use a 1/4 to 1/8 ounce diver. Silver is best on sunny days and in clear water, but if it's overcast or the water is murky, try a hot color like chartreuse. During a cold front, try trolling a small twister jig instead of a crankbait." McCadams recommends casting the plug out behind the boat, peeling an extra half-castlength of line off the spool, then using your outboard or electric motor to troll slowly through the school.

Casting jigs is another good route to slab prespawn crappie, the guide said. "After dropping marker buoys close to isolated cover along the migration route, target-cast with small twister or paddle-tail grubs, pretty much the way you'd cast to bass holding on objects."

PRESPAWN CRAPPIE IN A NUTSHELL

- Crappie begin migrating from deep to shallow water when the water approaches 50 degrees.

- They move toward their spawning grounds via a network of migration routes, including creek channels, ditches and banks associated with points.

- Crappie often pause at key spots along their migration routes to "stage" or hold until conditions are ideal for spawning.

- Key staging areas include bends in channels and ditches, and isolated cover occurring along these migration routes.

- Crappie may also stage in open water, especially in tributaries and coves. Here they may gather in large numbers to suspend, often near baitfish schools.

- A topo map, graph and set of marker buoys is essential to locate migrating/staging crappie.

- A mixture of live baits, lures and presentations that probe the bottom half of the water column will usually take prespawners.

Garry Mason's prespawn crappie game plan is much like that used by bass tournament anglers: targeting scattered wood cover along migration routes with artificial lures.

SUPERSIZE SPRING CRAPPIE

Every spring, hordes of fishermen converge on our nation's crappie waters to cash in on the annual spawning run. Many of these eager anglers have a fill-the-freezer mentality. They're out there strictly to load their coolers with tasty fillets, and that's fine. After all, crappie are an abundant resource, and few fish can compete as table fare.

But there are a growing number of *sport* crappie fishermen, folks who would rather catch a few big fish than a boatload of keepers. A single crappie the size as a Buick's hubcap would make their season, let alone their day.

Big crappie are more abundant on many of our lakes and reservoirs than ever, thanks to vigorous stocking programs and enlightened management practices, including stricter size and bag limits. But these superior fish can be maddeningly evasive and downright difficult to catch by conventional meat-fishing methods.

Enter Garry Mason. His passion is *BIG* crappie. His methods, described below in his own words, will seem radical to most long-time crappie fishermen, more like those of a pro bass angler, perhaps. But if trophy-sized crappie are your dream, and if you're not too set in your ways to put Mason's approach into practice, read and heed what follows. Your catch is about to be *supersized!* — *Don Wirth*

Migration Routes

On Kentucky Lake, as well as on most other well-known crappie venues nationwide, the typical spring approach is somewhat of a no-brainer. You park on sunken brushpiles, stake beds and other spawning habitat, fish vertically with minnows or tube jigs, and load the boat with eatin'-sized fish. Occasionally you'll catch a big crappie, but smaller fish are much more likely to be encountered. On a good day, it's not unusual for you and a companion to boat in excess of 50 average-sized papermouths.

So what could possibly be wrong with that? Plenty, if you're after big crappie. Years on the water have taught me that you're unlikely to tangle with exceptional fish by using traditional methods.

I'm convinced awareness of the crappie's spring migration routes is the first key to catching the biggest fish.

Most anglers seem to have the mistaken notion that in spring, crappie miraculously appear on their spawning beds from out of nowhere. They're willing to sit for days over a likely bedding spot in a shallow cove or tributary arm, hauling water until the fish magically show up. But in reality, crappie follow fairly predictable routes from deep to shallow water in spring, and I've found the biggest fish stick to these routes the closest. If you sit and wait for the fish to come to you, you're missing out on those fat pre-spawn slabs: huge, popeyed females heavy with eggs, and hyper-aggressive males eager to court them.

Think of a crappie's spring migration route as a corridor or highway from deep, open water to shallow, more sheltered areas suitable for spawning. Figure 1 shows a typical Kentucky Lake migration route. Usually around the first of March, our crappie are in 12 to 25 feet of water (depending on such factors as severity of our winter, lake level, etc.) and hanging around main-lake structures such as dropoffs, junctures of creek and river channels, etc. Often these fish are in large schools, suspended over deep cover or a structural edge.

As the water slowly warms into the upper 50's, a few fish break off from the pack and begin traveling a path toward their eventual bedding areas. I've found the biggest crappie are the first to make this move — being the superior members of their species, it may be genetically implanted in them to get to the best spawning grounds first. Now is the time to catch the crappie of a lifetime.

Rest Stops

Like tourists traveling an interstate highway, crappie visit several "rest stops" or staging areas as they migrate toward their spawning grounds. These holding places provide food, shelter and a brief respite from travel, and it's here where I catch many of my biggest crappie of the season.

Normally their first stop is a primary point at the mouth of a tributary. The best initial staging points are long and slow-tapering, ideally with some gravel on them. These points should also have some scattered wood cover, either natural wood such as stumps or laydown logs, or stake beds and brushpiles, cover that was intentionally placed there to attract crappie. Usually by the first of March you can hop from one primary point to another and catch 2 or 3 big crappie here, perhaps as many as 8 to 10 there.

Which brings up one of the biggest misconceptions about spring crappie — many anglers believe they move to the shallows en masse. Not so. Normally several fish will break off from the pack and begin migrating to shallower staging areas; then a few more will follow, and so on until most of the school is staging. This movement takes place in waves, the initial wave usually consisting of the biggest fish. Normally you'll begin catching these early arrivals on long points in 8 to 12 feet of water when the lake hits 60 degrees.

Once crappie begin moving up via those long points, they continue their shallow sojourn by following the old creek channel, man-made ditches, natural contours along the lake bottom and other pathways, stopping to hold around scattered wood cover. The biggest crappie feed aggressively when they're staging (probably to fuel up for the rigors of spawning) and are surprisingly easy to catch if you know where to look for them. With warming water, the migration continues farther back into the creek, where crappie pause to stage on secondary points (often with a fast taper into the creek channel), humps with brushy cover, or subtle dips and rises associated with flats. As the water temperature rises into the upper 60s, the fish will progress farther back into the shallows until they eventually reach suitable spawning spots.

Isolated wood cover plays a vital role in the staging process. During the prespawn period, the biggest crappie will consistently hold around relatively small, easily overlooked pieces of wood cover occurring along migration routes. This again goes against the mind-set of most crappie fishermen, who typically target the biggest brush-piles and stake beds they can find. I feel one reason relatively few big crappie are caught from large piles of cover is that they tend to draw a great many fish, most of which are small to average in size; these fish are often quicker to grab a minnow or jig than the superslabs.

During prespawn, look for wood cover on primary points, ledges and creek channel drops in the 8 to 12 foot range. Less is more. The cover you're after could be a single stump, the remnants of a brushpile or a few stakes driven into the lake bottom by some grizzled guide years ago; the important thing is that it's small in mass and isolated from other cover. Big crappie will gravitate to these bits of scattered wood like iron filings to a magnet, but most fishermen will either overlook it or not bother to fish it if they do notice it.

MASON'S ELECTRONICS SETUP

I've rigged the electronics on my 21-foot Triton guide boat to help me zero in on these migration routes and the obscure pieces of staging cover that occur on them. The primary link in the chain is a Pinpoint 3700 foot-control trolling motor. This has 5 transducers mounted on the bottom of the motor which send signals to a widescreen Pinpoint 7500 sonar unit. The transducers give me a choice of 3 different perspectives on the screen, or I can combine all 3 views into 1 if I like. The graph is mounted on a tall pedestal so it can be easily viewed when I'm standing up. The motor's foot control has a 16-foot extension cable, allowing me to operate it from virtually anywhere in the boat.

The neat thing about the Pinpoint trolling motor/graph is that they'll automatically track a preset depth contour. Let's say I've located a dropoff from 8 to 18 feet and want the boat to move along the structure at the 12-foot mark. I'll move out until I'm in 12 feet of water, push a button, and the trolling motor, working in conjunction with the graph, automatically moves the boat along the 12-foot contour at whatever speed I select. This is absolutely perfect for fishing spring migration routes.

Also mounted on the bow is a Lowrance X28 graph; its transducer shoots through the hull 5 feet from the nose of the boat. When I'm working my way down a contour and see some wood cover on the Pinpoint graph, I'll watch for it to appear on the Lowrance unit a second or two later; when it does, I'll drop a marker buoy on the cover and fish it.

Prespawn Approach

My early spring approach is more like bass fishing than crappie fishing. I seldom anchor or sit in one spot, rather I'm constantly on the move. Usually if I don't get a hit or catch a fish in my first 5 casts to a likely staging area, I'm outa there. Most of the other crappie fishermen who see me go down a bank probably think I'm competing in a bass tournament; they figure there's no way I could be fishing for crappie and moving that fast.

While most crappie addicts use minnows, I use lures exclusively for spring slabs. My bread and butter bait is a 2-inch Charlie Brewer Slider Grub, chartreuse in color, with a red, white or chartreuse Gripper Baits 1/16 ounce ball head jig. The Slider grub has a hard-throbbing paddle tail, which I'm convinced triggers a more positive response from big crappie during pre- and postspawn than either a curly-tail grub or tube jig.

I fish the Slider Grub and other lures I'll mention momentarily on a 7-foot Lamiglass 702 ultralight spinning rod, coupled with a

Shimano 1000 reel spooled with 6 lb. Berkley Solar XT monofiliment. This line is chartreuse in color; I'm positive it serves as an attractor for curious crappie. They notice the line, move closer to check it out, then see the grub go by and nail it.

The long, limber rod allows extra-long casts (routinely 40 feet +) with lightweight lures, another important factor. Big crappie are aggressive, yet spooky during prespawn; I like to stay a good distance from my targets. After I've marked wood cover along the migration route with a buoy, I'll cast well beyond the marker, count the lure down several feet, then swim it slowly and steadily back to the boat. Don't try to hop, skip or jump the lure; just turn the reel handle and let the tail do the work.

Counting down is critical, for there are often several big crappie holding near the staging cover at a precise depth. These fish often suspend over or around the wood, and their depth is easy to pattern if you count as the lure falls. When you get a strike at, say, a 4-count, you can to move to other similar places around the lake and catch 'em at the same depth.

People who don't think crappie put up much of a fight have never caught a superslab on an ultralight rig. These fish will load on like a freight train. I can't tell you how many die-hard bass fishermen I've converted to crappie after they tussled with a few big ones.

Speaking of bass, I've caught a surprising number of these critters on my crappie gear during prespawn, including largemouths exceeding 7 pounds and smallmouths over 5. Not to mention big sauger, shellcrackers, drum, even catfish. Fish migration routes correctly and you'll get your string stretched by all kinds of fish.

I stay with the Slider Grub 80% of the time, but in the first stages of migration, when the water is cold and fish are deep, I may use a leadhead with a tiny spinner. A little flash goes a long way when crappie are lethargic. Also, if the water is unusually muddy, I've had good luck on a twist-tail grub in a hot color like fuchsia. A 1/8 oz. bass spinnerbait works surprisingly well in muddy conditions, too; trim the skirt off in back of the hook, slow-roll it around wood and big crappie will nail it.

Spawn Time

The biggest crappie will start spawning when the water hits about 68 degrees, perhaps earlier if the weather has been mild and stable. They typically spawn around brushy cover in the backs of creek arms and sheltered bays in 2 to 5 feet of water, although this depth may vary with changes in lake level and water clarity.

Look for smaller brushpiles rather than huge masses of cover for the biggest spawners. I often find these around boat docks in creek arms. An unlikely spot that can produce big fish is an old bridge abutment in a shallow tributary; brush will pack against this during floods, providing a super spawning spot.

Spawn-time is the only time I'll do much vertical fishing. Now, tube jigs dropped straight under the boat into cover get eaten repeatedly, but you often have to fish your way through a zillion small fish to catch a single big one. Fortunately for me, superslabs don't hang around their spawning beds long. They hit it and quit it, then begin their migration back to deep water, using the same staging areas where you caught 'em in prespawn to stop and gorge themselves prior to returning to the main lake. Once they're off the bed, I fish for them with the same lures and approaches I used in prespawn, and can count on a couple more weeks of excellent migration-route pattern fishing before they disperse into the depths.

Things to Remember

Here are a few assorted tidbits of information to file away when you're after big spring crappie:

1. If you caught fish at a certain spot along their migration route one day and can't locate them the next, follow the contour or structural edge shallower. Exception: If crappie were on a primary point, they may move straight across the creek mouth to the opposing point. If they aren't on either point, they may be suspending in open water or on a hump or rockpile between the two points.

2. The migration route often doesn't follow the shoreline. Big crappie may move up on a primary point, follow it as it curls around, then pick up a ledge, channel lip or other depth contour to continue their shallow migration.

3. Big crappie will only move as far back into the creek arm as necessary to find a good spawning spot. For example, if the water shallows from 8 to 5 feet, then remains 5 feet deep for a long distance, they'll usually spawn at the first 5-foot water they encounter.

4. Keep moving. Don't spend more than a couple minutes casting to a single piece of cover.

5. Like bass, big crappie hold tighter to wood cover during frontal conditions. Make sure your lure bumps the cover.

6. If you get hung up, don't pull so hard that you dislodge the cover — it'll run off big fish. Break off, retie, and fish the spot again a little later.

7. Check likely staging spots several times during the course of the day, as fish routinely move on and off them.

8. Check light line for abrasions and retie often. Big crappie are fighters. And you never known when you might hang a lunker bass.

9. Selective harvest is critical when hunting supersized crappie. Releasing most of the big ones you catch will help ensure more trophy-class fish in your future.

SINKING COVER

By strategically sinking wood cover along likely migration routes, you can create super spring staging areas for big crappie.

Mason puts out cover in the form of stake beds and brushpiles when the reservoir is at winter pool, normally in February. Because he doesn't want other anglers to find his cover, he sinks it on cold, rainy days when few boats are on the lake.

Garry sinks cover at various depths along likely crappie migration routes from deep to shallow water, keying on primary points with a slow taper, 8-12 foot depth contours in tributary arms, humps, fast-dropping secondary points, etc. Keeping in mind that the lake level will rise around 5 feet by post-spawn, he sinks brushpiles so they'll be 8 feet or deeper, stake beds 8 feet or shallower, at summer pool. By varying the depth of the cover, Mason has staging spots he can fish throughout the entire spring period, regardless of water temperature or lake level.

Stake beds are vertical structures. Mason drives 1 1/2-inch hardwood stakes from 4 to 6 feet long into the lake bottom to form a bed approximately 10 feet x 12 feet. Brushpiles are horizontal structures. The guide sinks fruit tree branches "about as thick as your arm," weighting them down with concrete blocks. He may overlap more branches on top of some he's already sunk to form an X.

It's critical to sink cover so you can have some wood to fish regardless of wind direction. Otherwise if all of your cover is on the north side of the lake and the wind blows 20 mph out of the south, you're screwed.

Once you've dropped your cover, mark its position on a topo map or, ideally, a GPS unit.

Mason sinks around 20 stake beds and brushpiles per season. It's tedious and potentially dangerous work; always wear your life jacket, bring a buddy along to help, and exercise extreme caution. Of course, make sure your local regulations permit sinking cover.

A stake bed on Priest Lake, Tennessee.

TRICKS FOR PINPOINTING POSTSPAWN CRAPPIE

Crappie fishing during the spring spawning season has been described as a no-brainer. Just idle into the back of a reservoir tributary until you see an armada of boats, drop anchor around a fish attractor or stake bed, and start pulling in fish after fish after fish. What this approach lacks in finesse, it makes up for in efficiency. Anyone with a bucket of minnows or a bag of tube baits can score a cooler full of crappie when they're stacked up on their spawning grounds.

Fortunately, crappie are abundant throughout much of their range, so the species can withstand a few weeks of meat-fishing in most lakes. Besides, most of the cooler-packers only bother to fish in spring, and hang up their poles once the spawning cycle is over.

But serious crappie anglers don't limit their fishing to the spring spawn. They study the movements of their favorite gamefish year-'round, including the postspawn period. I asked three of the nation's best crappie tacticians to share their knowledge of postspawn crappie habits, and offer suggestions for tapping into quality fish during this often-tough transitional phase. Their input will help you find and catch more crappie once our favorite fish have vacated their spawning beds.

Garry Mason's Strategies

Garry Mason is on the water year-'round, and knows the postspawn period can be difficult…but not impossible. "Most anglers think of crappie as a schooling fish, but postspawn is the exception to this rule," Mason said. "During postspawn, you're targeting individual fish instead of members of a vast school. I jokingly tell my prespawn clients that we're going bass fishing, not crappie fishing, and in many respects, the approaches that work best now for both species are identical."

While crappie usually bite aggressively when schooled up on their spawning beds, they can get lockjaw following the spawn, the guide has found. "Many anglers get frustrated during this period because they had gotten used to finding big schools of actively-feeding fish packed tight around spawning cover earlier in the year, then suddenly the schools break up and the fish scatter. But if you're patient, you can put together a pattern that will continue to produce quality crappie, and plenty of 'em."

The postspawn crappie angler's success hinges on mobility and versatility, Mason said. "Now is not the time to fish any one spot for long periods of time, even a place where you've caught fish in the past," he stressed. "As when competing in a late spring bass tournament, you'll catch more fish now if you stay on the move, hitting similar key spots spread over a fairly wide area. Typically each spot will yield one or two fish, not great numbers of crappie." The

TRICKS FOR PINPOINTING POSTSPAWN CRAPPIE

moody nature of postspawn fish can make them reluctant to bite standard presentations after their bedding cycle is completed, he added: "Often you have to show 'em something totally different to coax them into hitting." More on Mason's postspawn lures and presentations in a moment.

Garry begins the postspawn period by fishing shallow areas that crappie use as migration routes from their spawning grounds to the main lake. "Crappie will follow a path connecting the main body of a reservoir to their spring spawning areas," he explained. "In early spring, they'll often stage in large numbers on a tributary point, then gradually work their way into the back-end of the tributary arm as the water warms, following structures such as bluff banks, ledges, creek channels or depth contours. Once they're done spawning, they'll reverse their route and work their way back to main lake structures, including river channel dropoffs, humps and points, where they'll spend the summer."

Garry said a shoreline adjacent to a large concentration of brushpiles, stake beds or fish attractors is a good place to start looking for crappie in postspawn. "They'll be fairly shallow, often 2 to 4 feet, after spawning, which makes them highly susceptible to a lure presentation. Usually they'll be sitting around isolated wood cover, such as a lone stump or submerged bush. I'll often start with a Charlie Brewer Slider Grub on a 1/8 ounce Slider Head jig; this is rigged below a small slip bobber and cast into shallow water. I'll work the rig back to the boat slowly, trying to make the sinker pop and gurgle as it comes through the water – this can attract curious crappie, and occasionally a nice bass as well. If the fish are deeper than 6 feet, I'll remove the slip bobber and cast just the Slider grub, swimming it back to the boat with a slow, constant retrieve. If I don't get bit up shallow, I'll move out progressively deeper until I contact fish."

According to Mason, wild jighead and grub colors work great in postspawn – florescent pink and hot orange are his favorites. A small in-line spinner such as a #2 Mepps Black Fury is deadly now as well. "Whatever lure you use, retrieve it slowly," he cautioned. "Crappie are seldom aggressive in postspawn, but will strike a slow-moving lure presented close to cover."

As the water continues to warm, Mason follows shorelines and depth contours progressively farther from the shallows toward the mouth of the tributary. "During postspawn, some crappie will be in the back of the creek arm, others in the middle, still others near the mouth, another reason for covering as much water as possible now," he said.

Jim Duckworth's Tactics

"Crappie are often lethargic immediately after spawning, which can be expected when you consider the stress that the reproductive ritual places on their metabolic processes," Jim Duckworth said. "However, since not all crappie spawn at the same time, you're likely to encounter some highly aggressive fish along with some sluggish ones during this period. You never really know what mood they'll be in on any given spot, but to be on the safe side, a slow to moderate retrieve usually produces best."

Jim has found that after crappie leave their brushy spawning habitat, they'll often chill out for a few days by holding along a nearby breakline such as a dropoff or channel lip in the 7 to 10 foot zone.. "In shallow reservoirs with plenty of flooded bushes, crappie will move to the outside edges of the shrubbery after spawning," he indicated. "I used to be a full-time commercial diver, and I can't tell you how many times I've seen crappie parking along these brushy breaklines in late spring, often suspending right over a bush or stump. You can retrieve a lure a foot from 'em and they'll ignore it, but careen it off wood and they'll bite. Fortunately, crappie regain their strength fairly quickly after the procreation process, and will actively resume chasing small minnows within a few days."

Duckworth often trolls during postspawn. "Trolling around 2 mph lets you cover a lot of water efficiently, desirable when crappie are scattered about in sparse numbers as they often are now. I troll 200-series Bandit crankbaits on 8 pound line — this approach is deadly on suspending fish, which often grab the passing lure with a reaction strike. Run crankbaits up to 1 1/2 cast-lengths behind the boat along tributary breaklines. It'll help if you scout these spots before you start fishing and drop marker buoys to delineate the dropoff."

The Tennessee guide finds murky lakes produce far better than clear lakes during postspawn: "For some reason, crappie bite more readily now when they rely on their lateral lines to feed instead of their eyes. In the Middle Tennessee area where I fish, I always do better at Old Hickory Reservoir, which is pretty stained, than Center Hill Reservoir, which is gin-clear."

STEVE MCCADAM'S METHODS

Steve McCadams has built a successful career through his ability to put his clients on quality fish regardless of the season. But even this master angler acknowledges that the postspawn period can be challenging. "Normally if you can locate crappie, you can catch them fairly easily, but postspawn is the exception to this rule," he said. "The fish are usually exhausted from the spawning ritual. Their bodies are going through major hormonal changes, and chasing a minnow is often the farthest thing from their minds."

McCadams points out that to further complicate the issue, the post-spawn period is not that well-defined. "Spawning takes place in waves when the water temperature hits around 62 degrees," he explained. "At any given time, there will be some crappie in a pre-spawn mode, others in the process of spawning, still others that have completed the spawn and left the nest. Many crappie will spawn in the 62 to 66 degree range, but there are always some late spawners when the lake hits 70 degrees. This in turn impacts when fish transition into a postspawn pattern. But normally by the time the lake hits 75 degrees, mid-May in my area, most crappie are postspawners."

Immediately after spawning, male crappie often remain near the nest for a short period of time, either to guard the eggs from predator bluegill, or to feed on fry that hatch, McCadams said. Female crappie usually back off the nest and suspend.

Steve finds most of his postspawn fish on flats in large tributary bays as well as on the main lake. "Postspawn is the one time when crappie aren't closely associated with wood cover, either big concentrations of brush or scattered stumps," he said. "Most of the fish are so stressed out from spawning that they just want to hang out in open water and recuperate. I see many crappie on my graph during postspawn suspending 12 to 15 feet deep in 20 feet of water, just hanging over a slick flat with very little cover on it. These fish are in a true transitional mode between their spring and summer patterns."

The best postspawn flats are on a migration route with an easy to shallow, brushy spawning areas and deep main-lake structures, the guide said. "The flat may appear featureless, but there's probably a channel dropoff, ledge or ditch out at the end of the structure."

Slow trolling with multi-pole spider rigs is McCadams' recommend approach in postspawn. "The crappie are going to be fairly deep and scattered now, and you'll contact more fish by covering as much water as possible. The spider rig approach lets you present a buffet of baits and lures near the bottom, middle and top of the water column, all at the same time, and all at a slow speed, which is extra-important due to the sluggish nature of the fish."

Tubes 'n tuffies – that's the ticket in postspawn, Steve continued. "The bite can change from one hour to the next – they may want chartreuse tubes at 8 a.m., pink tubes at 9 and minnows at 10. It's really important to change colors and presentation depths often if you aren't getting bites, 'cause you often have to trigger postspawn crappie into biting."

DOWNSIZE FOR POSTSPAWN CRAPPIE

Let's not kid ourselves – postspawn crappie can be a tough nut to crack. Our favorite fish are often suspended, scattered and stressed from spawning. Steve McCadams suggests taking a page from the tournament bass angler's textbook to improve your postspawn crappie catch: "Whenever the bass bite gets tough, the savvy angler downsizes his tackle. This approach works for crappie in postspawn, too. Use the smallest minnows you can find, the runts that you'd normally pitch into the lake from your bucket. Or, fish tiny marabou jigs or miniature twister grubs. If you were fishing 8 pound line, drop back to 6, even 4 – abrasion isn't a major factor now, since many fish are suspending on slick flats with little wood cover. And above all, use a slow, patient presentation."

POSTSPAWN CRANKBAIT TROLLING

I was wrapping up an article for a bass fishing magazine when the phone rang. "Get your backside out of your office, meet me at the lake and let's go crappie fishing!" Jim Duckworth demanded.

"No way," I replied wearily. "I've got deadlines staring me in the face on stories I haven't even started yet. Besides, in case you haven't noticed, it's June. Crappie season's over. Call me next April, when we stand a chance of catching some decent fish for photos!"

"What if I told you I've been catching my limit every day for a week?" Duckworth continued. "And furthermore, what if I told you I was doing something a writer like you might call 'unorthodox' to catch 'em?"

"I'd never use the word 'unorthodox' — too many syllables," I corrected him. "And yes, I'll meet you at the boat ramp in 30 minutes."

I've fished with the best crappie guides in the country, and I thought I'd seen everything. But Jim Duckworth showed me a system for catching post-spawn crappie that hot June morning that's so effective, it's nothing short of amazing. It combines two concepts that will seem foreign to most crappie anglers: crankbaits and power trolling. If you're like I was and think the crappie season is history once the spawning run is over, Duckworth's system is guaranteed to turn your head around!

Dog-Days Dynamite

"I first got onto power trolling (trolling with a gas outboard as opposed to an electric motor) a couple years ago," Duckworth explained. "I was having lunch at a marina at Priest Lake near Nashville after a morning of bass fishing when I noticed some commotion outside on the dock. I looked out to see an elderly gentleman holding up the biggest stringer of crappie I'd seen in months. When the crowd around him dispersed, I offered to buy him a cheeseburger if he'd tell me how he'd caught 'em. He said he'd started out trolling crankbaits for saugeye, a sauger/walleye hybrid that's been stocked in the lake, but gave up on them once big crappie started banging his lures."

Duckworth has trolled crankbaits for years for white bass, sauger and walleye, but never for crappie; it took several weeks of experimentation for him to refine the technique. "Crappie don't relate to the bottom nearly as much as these other species do, especially during the post-spawn/early summer period," he said. "When running multiple lures, I found I'd consistently catch more and bigger crappie on crankbaits that probed the middle of the water column as opposed to the top or bottom quarters."

The guide discovered that crankbait trolling was sheer dynamite during the dreaded post-spawn period, when the lake has heated above 70 degrees and crappie have left their shallow spring haunts. "The main reason why so many people quit crappie fishing after the spawn is that these fish tend to scatter all over the place. When they're spawning, you can load the boat on a single brushpile or stake bed, but in post-spawn, you have to hunt and peck for a few fish. This is very time consuming with standard crappie presentation methods, but a no-brainer if you're trolling. It's the ultimate way to cover the maximum amount of water in the minimum amount of time."

Also, the post-spawn phase puts crappie in perfect position for a trolling presentation, Duck noted. "When they're spawning, they're shallow enough to catch by casting minnows under floats. Then when the water gets hot in midsummer, they're too deep for anything but bottom-bumping rigs. But in early summer, they're usually suspended in a zone that's easily probed by a crankbait."

Where to Troll

Duckworth begins his search for post-spawn crappie immediately adjacent to known spawning areas. "I know it's time to start trolling when about three weeks have passed since the water first hit the 65-degree mark," he explained. "Often the water temp will be in the low 70s then, but I've found that this three-week delay is a better gauge than the water temp. Normally most of the crappie in the lake will have spawned by then, and are slowly filtering out to the first dropoff they come to."

As a rule of thumb, Duckworth begins trolling in the back half of tributary arms. "The first places I catch crappie in post-spawn are approximately twice as deep as their spawning areas — 12 to 18 feet is a safe bet for most lakes," he said. "There's always a sudden depth change associated with this spot — crappie move out of their spawning areas via a ditch, depth contour, ledge or creek channel."

As the season progresses, fish will move out toward the mouth of the tributary, still suspending in the water column. "I've tested this pattern on all types of lakes in several states, and have usually found post-spawners to be somewhere within that magic 12 to 18 foot zone until the water gets downright hot," Duckworth indicated. "Once it does, they move out onto the main lake via the river channel and drop out of the range of a trolled crankbait."

Hotspots Duckworth looks for include the deep ends of gravel flats, areas with standing timber and downstream points at the mouths of tributaries. Of course, any area with suspended baitfish schools is a likely crappie magnet as well. "Always look for baitfish – no matter the season, they're the ultimate key to crappie location," the guide stated.

Jim scans the area he intends to fish with his graph, then sets out several marker buoys at 10-foot depth intervals to delineate dropoffs. Trolling is seldom done in a straight line, but rather in a lazy S pattern. "This facilitates tremendous water coverage, and causes your lures to change speed when your make a turn, which often triggers strikes.," he said. Jim tries to follow the depth change along its course as he trolls, for he knows crappie often suspend over the dropoff.

BOAT SETUP

Duckworth fishes from a 20-foot aluminum boat which he designed and built himself (he's a master welder). It's powered by a 200-horse Honda four-stroke outboard, a low-emission power plant capable of trolling all day at speeds of around 2 1/2 mph without loading up.

POSTSPAWN CRANKBAIT TROLLING

If you don't have one of the new 'green' outboards like a Honda or Mercury OptiMax, you'll need a small "kicker" motor, preferably 9 to 15 hp, for trolling. A big, conventional 2-cycle outboard is not well suited to this technique, for its spark plugs become fouled when it operates for extended periods at low rpm.

Electronics are ultra-important when trolling ,Jim emphasized. "I use both a conventional graph and a GPS unit trolling," he said. "They allow me to monitor boat speed, water temp, bottom features and depth at the same time. The graph has a wide-angle transducer mounted on the transom. I put the GPS on tracking mode, which lays out a plotted trail of where I've been and allows me to retrace my path precisely."

Adjustable rod holders are an important part of the equation. ""You must be able to adjust the rod tip up or down; this helps keep lines from tangling and lets you compensate for the depths different lures are capable of running," he said. "When I'm with a client, I generally run four rods. Rods rigged with the deepest-running lures are placed in holders at the port and starboard corners of the transom; these are adjusted so the rods are at a 45 degree angle from the stern. I generally run 100 feet of line off the back rods. Then I run two more rods rigged with shallower-running lures off the sides of the boat, adjacent to the console. These are placed in holders positioned at a 90 degree angle to the gunwales, with their tips parallel to the water. I use 6 1/2 and 7 foot medium action All Pro graphite baitcasting rods for trolling; these have just the right amount of shock absorption for this application. A rod that's too stiff will rip the hooks out of a crappie; one that's too light won't hook as many fish." Duckworth mates his rods with high-speed baitcasting reels spooled with 8 to 12 pound Trilene XT, test depending on crappie depth, water color and amount of snaggy cover present. He keeps the drag set extra-light — it must give under 3 to 4 pounds of pressure, or papermouthed crappie will tear free.

When a fish strikes, Jim lets the rod set the hook. "I cringe when I see a client grab the rod and rear back when a crappie hits," he said. "Invariably the hook tears out of its mouth. I use a net to land every fish; you'll lose 30% of the crappie you hook while trolling if you don't net them, because their mouths are almost always torn by the crankbait's hooks. Just pick up the rod from its holder, reel line in at a constant medium speed and ease the fish into the net. Try to bulldog the fish to the boat and it'll usually rip off."

Lures to Try

Duckworth's extensive experimentation with power trolling has shown that certain crankbaits outshine others for big crappie. "My favorites are medium-diving Bandit plugs; these always run true, dive to predictable depth levels and don't cost you an arm and a leg. The latter is very important because you can count on losing at least a couple crankbaits a day in a snaggy-bottomed reservoir, even with a good plug knocker." Similar small- to medium-sized diving plugs, the same ones favored by smallmouth bass anglers, will also work. I avoid the larger potbellied bass divers; crappie will occasionally hit them but they tend to run below the level the fish are using during post-spawn, and have a habit of tangling up in bottom cover," Jim said.

When Duckworth spots a good school of crappie on his graph, he'll troll a tandem rig he uses in the spring for white bass. "Attach a 12-inch leader to the rear hook of a crankbait and tie a white or chartreuse twist-tail grub rigged on a 1/8 ounce jighead to the tag end. Often you'll pick up two crappie at once."

MORE TROLLING SAVVY

- Using a swivel when trolling greatly reduces line twist.

- Check your crankbaits near the boat to make sure they're running true before letting out a lot of line.

- Rivers can be surprisingly good in hot weather, for they tend to run much cooler than lakes. Troll crankbaits along gravel bars for crappie, white bass and other species. Since rivers are murky and highly-oxygenated, expect crappie to be 50% shallower there than in a lake.

- Always use abrasion-resistant line with ample stretch when trolling, and check it frequently for rough spots.

- Keep a big selection of crankbait color patterns on hand. When beginning the fishing day, always run lures of different patterns, replacing colors that catching fish with those that are. Normally in post-spawn, shad patterns (chrome, silver, blue) work well in clear to slightly stained water, especially on sunny days. In murky water, and on cloudy days, bright colors such as chartreuse or orange often catch more fish.

- If you aren't catching fish, maybe you're trolling too deep. In early summer, crappie often hang tight to baitfish schools scattered across the top third of the water column. A shallow-diver may be the ticket to filling your livewell.

Legendary Tennessee guide Harold Morgan knows there's more than one way to catch springtime crappie.

FRESH STRATEGIES FOR SPRING SLABS

Spring crappie fishing has traditionally been a matter of dunking live minnows or tube jigs around submerged spawning cover. This tried-and-true strategy usually works – if it didn't, why would everybody be doing it?

But there are drawbacks to this popular spring crappie approach. Often there are so many anglers vying for the same spots, you have to take a number to fish them. Unless you're lucky enough to tap into the right tree, the fish seldom run very big on this pattern. And perhaps most vexing of all, doing the same thing in the same places, year after year after year, can get downright boring!

I say, thank goodness there are crappie anglers out there who aren't afraid to color outside the lines when developing their spring strategies! They give the rest of us new tactics to try when those "old reliable" patterns fail…and they remind us of the importance of experimentation and creative thinking in our angling approaches.

Here, our guides share their favorite off-the-wall approaches for spawn-time crappie. These strategies are guaranteed to excite a bite from jaded crappie, and will breathe new life into your spring fishing.

JIGS ON PEA GRAVEL & SAND

When Harold Morgan talks crappie fishing, savvy anglers listen. The amiable guide is renowned for his brush-beating, vertical-fishing approaches involving multiple live baits or jigs fished with a heavy sinker. No wonder I was more than a little surprised when he told me about his latest spring tactic.

Check this out: while other anglers are jammed into the backs of tributaries fishing flooded cover, Morgan and his clients have been quietly reeling in monster slabs by targeting bare sand and pea gravel flats, bars and points! "I got on this approach five years ago, but have been reluctant to talk about it because it's contrary to what every crappie fisherman, myself included, has always believed about crappie only spawning on wood," Morgan explained. "There's little or no wood where I'm fishing, but I'm convinced these fish are spawning nonetheless . The sand and gravel structures I do best on are usually located only a few casts from submerged stake beds and brushpiles. I believe crappie have been driven to these slick areas by excessive fishing pressure on their usual woody spots."

Harold says crappie on this weird pattern are usually shallow, and readily bite small tube and twister jigs…provided they're presented with this curious twist: "I pinch a bobber on the line 3 to 4 feet above the jig, cast the rig onto the sand or gravel structure, then reel it moderately fast so the jig stays at a 45-degree angle as it trails behind the float," he explained. "I've experimented a great deal with retrieves, and keeping the float/jig combination moving consistently outscores a stop-and-go retrieve on the lakes I'm fishing. Of course, this may not be the case on your home waters, so always experiment with retrieve speed to see what the fish want."

Here's more good news: this pattern even works during spring cold fronts, Morgan said. "If a front blows through and I'm not contacting fish with the float 3 feet above the jig, I'll slide it up to 4 or 5 feet until I start getting bites. Usually the crappie haven't moved far and are suspending out over the deep edge of the structure."

Spinnerbaits for Slabs

The spinnerbait is arguably the most popular bass lure ever created. Weekend fishermen and tournament pros alike use these flashy, hard-throbbing artificials to snatch lunker largemouths from stumps and brushy cover.

Garry Mason uses spinnerbaits, too. He casts a downsized version of this deadly lure into areas where crappie are waxing romantic, and often hauls in some surprisingly big fish while other anglers are hauling water.

"While most artificial lures try to mimic an injured minnow, a spinnerbait swims like a live minnow," Mason explained. "By simply retrieving the lure slowly and steadily, its blade(s) reflect light and emit vibrations like a lively baitfish. What could possibly be more appetizing to a predatory fish like a crappie? It's the best strike-triggering lure I've ever fished. You'll catch slabs on spinnerbaits even when they've turned off live bait."

Of course, the spinnerbaits bass anglers throw are way too big for crappie. Mason uses a miniature Little Gripper spinnerbait with a head that weighs a mere 1/32 ounce; this finesse lure has a single, tiny teardrop-shaped Colorado blade. He'll often remove the rubber skirt from the lure and thread a 2-inch Slider grub on the hook instead. "This reduces the mass of the presentation a bit, and works especially well during spring cold fronts," Garry noted.

Mason casts the tiny spinnerbait on a light-action 7-foot spinning rod, targeting brush, stake beds, stumps and other classic staging and spawning cover. He's caught several crappie over 3 pounds on this approach, as well as the occasional big bass. His spinnerbaitin' advice to crappie anglers is simple and straightforward: "Just cast the lure a little beyond your target, reel it slowly and steadily back to the boat, and keep the livewell lid open."

Power Fishing

Jim Duckworth is on the water more than any angler I know, so I figured he could be counted on for an innovative springtime crappie approach. He calls his strategy "power fishing," and it's the fastest route to spring slabs you'll ever take. "I get a lot of strange looks from folks parked on brushpiles dunking jigs or minnows in the backs of tributary arms," Duckworth laughed. "They're not used to seeing a crappie fisherman cover so much water in such a short amount of time."

The guide motors to a shallow, brushy flat or bar, turns on his trolling motor, and doesn't shut it off until he's ready to run to another creek arm. "I put the trolling motor on low to medium speed and start casting a Slider Whirley Bee grub spinner or a 2-inch Slider grub," he explained. "If the water temperature is above 65 degrees, I put the boat in 8 feet of water and cast right to the bank; if it's 65 degrees or below, I move out a castlength or two so I'm throwing into 5 to 10 feet of water."

After the lure hits the water, Jim lets it fall all the way to the bottom, then slow-reels it back to his boat: "Putting too much rod action on your lure during the spawn season is a huge mistake; these fish want their meal fished s-l-o-w and easy, not hopping all over creation." On the odd day that a grub spinner or straight grub don't produce, the guide chunks a small Bandit crankbait, letting it bump off stumps and root bottom like a fleeing crawfish — this works especially well if the water is murky after a hard rain.

Keeping constantly on the move is the key to Duckworth's success with this pattern. "While everybody else is using a saturation approach, repeatedly jigging bait or lures into confined patches of cover, I'm using a shotgun approach for fish that are scattered out across bigger structures," he pointed out. "Some of these fish will be prespawn, others spawning, still others postspawn. The key is to get on a bank that has a well-defined dropoff around the 8 to 12 foot zone; crappie use this depth contour when moving in and out of spawning areas."

Duckworth finds his run-and-gun approach well-suited to first-time crappie anglers, especially kids. "Newcomers to our sport tend to get antsy when parking on a stake bed all day, but love the challenge of casting to constantly-changing targets," he pointed out.

Open-Water Float 'n Fly

The jig/bobber is versatile and deadly for crappie. Although Harold Morgan casts it on shallow flats and bars, Fred McClintock uses it immediately before the spawn as an open-water crappie tantalizer.

"Dale Hollow Reservoir where I fish is a canyon-type lake: deep, clear and rocky," he explained. "Here, winter bass fishermen often use a jig/bobber combo, known locally as the float 'n fly, for suspended smallmouths. I decided to try it for spring crappie, and it works!"

Wood cover is scare in Dale Hollow, and there are often boats parked on every isolated stickup and brushpile once the crappie move shallow to spawn. Rather than fight the crowds, McClintock targets open-water slabs en route to their spawning grounds. "These pre-spawn fish follow major tributary structures such as channel bluffs and ledges into the backs of the creek arms," he said. "They're usually suspending 8 to 12 feet deep, and the frequent cold fronts that blow through this region in spring can make them pretty lethargic. Soaking a tiny lure in front of their noses for an indefinite time period is a dependable way of catching them."

McClintock, an accomplished multi-species angler, dug deep into his tacklebox for some sinking trout flies when formulating his float 'n fly crappie approach. "I call these my lures of last resort; they sink very slowly and look more like an insect than a minnow. Crappie will eat 'em like candy in the toughest situations, including bright sunshine and frontal passages."

Fred fishes his finesse rig on a 9-foot ultralight spinning rod. He begins with the bobber 8 feet above the fly, then moves it deeper or shallower as the bite dictates. He uses what he calls a "non-retrieve," simply casting the rig around a bluff or over a deep ledge and letting wave action activate the bobber and fly.

Remember the Fundamentals

"Adding new tricks to your repertoire of crappie strategies is great as long as you don't neglect the fundamentals," Steve McCadams stressed. "When spring finally rolls around, many crappie anglers are so eager to hit the water and start hauling in fish that they overlook the basics that can spell the difference between a memorable catch and a poor one." McCadams listed the following as must-do's for a successful spring outing:

- *Strip it* — "Strip last year's gnarly, kinky line off your reels and start the season with fresh monofiliment. Remember that crappie fishing is a contact sport, and use abrasion-resistant line."

- *Sharp idea* — "Keep a file in your shirt pocket and never get in too big a hurry to touch up hook points. You'll stick a lot more light-biters if you do."

- *Stock up* — "Spring means rapidly-changing weather and water conditions. The lake may be clear one day, muddy the next. High winds and rapidly-moving cold fronts are givens. Make sure your jig selection covers all the bases. Before you start the spring season, visit your local tackle shop and stock up on a good supply of jig heads in weights from 1/8 to 1/32 ounces, and a selection of soft plastic tube baits, grubs and twisters in colors for both clear and murky water. Store them in a clear plastic utility box. Write the weights of the jigs on the lid with a waterproof marker."

- *Mark it* — "Keep a set of marker buoys handy. When you see a submerged brushpile or stake bed on your graph, toss out a marker near, but not directly on, the cover. This is especially helpful in open water, where wind drifts you away from fish-holding objects."

- *Angle of the dangle* – "To give your jigs a natural swimming appearance and avoid excessive hangups, the lure should hang at a 45-degree angle from the line. Each time you hook a fish or snag into cover, take a second to push the knot back behind the eyelet for the right presentation."

DROP-SHOTTING FOR CRAPPIE

Drop-shotting is the current craze among America's bass fishermen. This finesse method involves a sinker tied to the end of the line with an artificial lure, often a small plastic worm or soft jerk bait, tied 2 to 3 feet above the sinker. The angler drops the sinker to the bottom and lifts, lowers or shakes the rig repeatedly around likely bass-holding areas.

Seasoned crappie fishermen know a good thing when they see it, and some of them have borrowed the drop-shot technique and converted it into a deadly springtime crappie tactic. "Drop-shotting is an awesome technique for clear reservoirs, because it allows you to keep a small lure in the strike zone indefinitely when fishing prime crappie-holding structures such as deep brushpiles, channel dropoffs with stumps, and standing timber," Jim Duckworth said. He rigs his light-action baitcasting outfit with 12 pound fluorocarbon line, attaches a 1 ounce bell sinker to the tag end (3/4 ounce when fishing 10 feet deep or less) and ties 4-inch "drop lines" 1 and 3 feet above the weight. To these he attaches 2-inch Slider grubs rigged on 1/32-ounce heads.

FRESH STRATEGIES FOR SPRING SLABS

Jim positions his boat directly over his target, such as a channel dropoff or ditch lined with stumps, or a sunken brushpile or stakebed. "I drop the sinker right into the middle of the cover and shake the rod tip gently so the jig vibrates in place without hopping up and down," he said. "If I don't get a bite, I'll reel the sinker straight up a couple of feet, move down the bank with my trolling motor and lower and shake the rig again. Sooner or later I'll catch a fish – either that, or knock a big crappie on the head!" The fluorocarbon line Duckworth uses with his set-up is incredibly sensitive, and allows the angler to feel even the lightest tap in deep water.

If the vertical presentation doesn't ring the crappies' chimes, Jim will lay off the structure a bit, make a long cast with the drop-shot rig and simply reel slowly, dragging the sinker across the bottom. He keeps a set of marker buoys on the front deck of his boat; when he contacts a crappie, he kicks a marker into the lake so he can make repeated casts from the same spot.

Harold Morgan pioneered many of the methods of deep summer crappie fishing in use today.

LOAD UP ON DEEP SUMMER CRAPPIE

Talk about great crappie fishing, March, April and May were truly awesome. Crappie were stacked in shallow tributaries and bays on every brushpile, stake bed and logjam you could find. Action was non-stop — remember the day you and your buddy boated over a hundred fish?

Then suddenly, just like somebody threw a switch, the crappie were gone from the shallows. And like three-quarters of the nation's reservoir crappie anglers, you stashed your poles and minnow buckets in the attic until next spring.

Too bad, because you're missing out on some of the best crappie action of the year!

"Summer is my favorite crappie season of all," swears Harold Morgan. "But it demands a totally different style of fishing than spring."

Totally different, indeed. I followed Morgan around the lake to learn how he locates and catches mega-numbers of slab crappie during summer. His methods are unorthodox, but incredibly productive. And best of all, they'll work for you on your home waters.

Finding the Fish

"Here in Tennessee, fishing is easy in the shallows during April," Morgan said. "When the water is between 57 and 67 degrees, bedding crappie will hit a jig or minnow without hesitation. But after they spawn, crappie head out to deeper pastures, and can seem impossible to find. If you have patience, however, you can locate them and stay with 'em all summer long."

But you may have to suffer a bit first, Morgan laughed. "The period immediately following the spring spawn — May in my area, June if you live up north — is probably the worst time of the year for crappie. They're in what I call a 'distress mode,' strung out from the rigors of procreation. They don't want to bite, and they don't want to socialize. They feel like you feel when you don't get that morning cup of coffee."

Obviously the first puzzle you need to solve is finding the fish. This isn't as hard as you might think, Harold indicated. "After spawning, crappie move out of shallow tributary arms toward the main lake, usually following the old creek channel. As they travel, they hold around deep wood structure, especially trees left standing along the creek bank before the reservoir was formed. Many of these are in the 20 to 30 foot zone on my area reservoirs; yours may be a bit deeper or shallower."

The arrival of summer means heavy-duty structure fishing, which requires the proper boat setup. Morgan recommends two depth finders, one at the console and one at the bow. The transducer for the front unit should be mounted on your bow-mounted trolling motor. He runs two graphs up front, with both transducers mounted on the trolling motor. These are connected to different batteries so there's no interference. Finally, you'll need a half-dozen marker buoys to delineate offshore structures where crappie lurk.

Harold uses his big motor to idle out of a tributary arm. Moving in a lazy S pattern, he drops a marker each time he crosses the channel. Then he gets on his trolling motor and retraces his path, targeting deep trees, stumps and brushpiles lining the channel dropoff with small minnows or 1/32 ounce twister or tube jigs.

Vertical Presentation

You've already read about Morgan's "heavy metal" Kentucky rig. It's perfect for probing deep structure in summer. "Start the summer by fishing vertically," Harold advised. "Get directly over the tree with your trolling motor and lower the sinker all the way to the bottom, then reel up s-l-o-w-l-y. The bite is usually very tentative during the post-spawn, so be alert. If you get a bite, immediately mark your line with a waterproof marker so you can pinpoint that depth on future presentations." He indicated that crappie will seldom stack up in huge towers now; rather a smaller number of fish will be compressed at a specific depth on a specific piece of cover. "They might be 23 feet deep on the first tree you come to, 27 feet on the next. Fish often gather in loose schools at the base of the tree. You've got to be patient now, for you'll seldom find crappie on every tree during the post-spawn. In fact, you might probe 10 to 15 trees before you ever get a bite."

Morgan avoids anchoring now. "Crappie are hard enough to catch in the early summer transition as it is; dropping a 15-pound hunk of lead in their living room will only clamp their lips tighter," he said.

Hot Times

The guide finds the arrival of June (July up north) means awesome crappie fishing, even better than spring for both numbers and size. "By now, crappie have regrouped big-time," Morgan said. "Large numbers will be in the 15 to 25 foot zone; locally, I catch most of my fish at 20 feet. These fish are aggressive for the first time since the spawning season, and will bite readily once you find them."

Crappie will be schooled tightly on scattered wood cover located on main-lake structures, including river channel dropoffs, humps, long points and "plains" (deep flats adjacent to a channel drop). "The operative word now is 'scattered' — you'll want to avoid areas with thick tangles of cover, and concentrate instead on broad expanses of clean structure peppered with occasional pieces of wood," Morgan advised.

Harold relies on electric trolling to load his livewell in hot weather. His favorite structure is an offshore hump rising to 15 feet of the surface. He first idles over the structure and delineates it with marker buoys. Then he returns to open water and lets out between 30 and 40 feet of line on a heavy sinker rig. As the sinker drops, he turns his trolling motor on high and heads for the hump. "I slow down when I feel the sinker hit bottom, then speed up slightly," he explained. "The object is to keep the sinker tapping bottom occasionally, but not dragging. If you don't feel bottom, slow down until you do. If you drag bottom, speed up until you don't. Never let your boat come to a complete stop — keep moving!"

LOAD UP ON DEEP SUMMER CRAPPIE

Keep a sharp eye on your graph, Morgan said. "If you spot a tree or brushpile on the bottom, adjust your speed so your trolled rig comes close to it, even bumps it, but doesn't hang in it. The pear-shaped bell sinkers I prefer are designed to minimize hangups; if you feel your rod load up as your sinker drags over sunken wood, speed up quickly and it'll will often slip through the branches. Some hangups are inevitable; I keep leaders pretied and extra sinkers handy so I can get back into the battle quickly after breaking off."

This slow/fast/slow presentation causes your baits or lures to rise and fall in an extremely enticing manner, the guide explained. "Many bites occur as your rig bumps cover, but summer crappie will fool you — they might be ganged up close to bottom *between* scattered pieces of wood. When you catch a good fish from a certain spot, try vertical fishing — chances are there's a whole gang of crappie down there."

Using multiple rods pays off in midsummer. "When I'm guiding clients, I run two bottom-bumping rigs with heavy sinkers, a mid-depth line with a split shot, and a shallow line with no weight at all," Harold noted. "This is a tremendous way to locate large concentrations of fish quickly — usually one depth zone will hold the lion's share of the fish on any given day."

It's easy to stay so focused on the bottom that you ignore the upper portion of the water column. "Around mid-morning in summer, large numbers of crappie often rise slowly to within 8 or 10 feet of the surface in a dense cloud," Morgan said. "It's easy to mistake these fish for a school of bait; run your graph in the manual mode and adjust the sensitivity until you can make out the crappie. Shallow, suspending crappie are very spooky and tough to catch — the best tactic is to drop a jig or minnow well below the pack, then reel up through them slowly. This produces far better than dropping an offering down to their level and soaking it in front of their faces."

Shifting-Patterns

As summer progresses, expect to see these patterns change gradually, Morgan predicted. "On some days, especially by mid-August here in Tennessee, crappie will be super-deep — I've taken them down to 46 feet. These fish may be relating to the thermocline; they're usually suspending, but still catchable if you lower a bait below them and reel up through them."

When summer finally begins to wind down, crappie will start a gradual migration to the upper end of the reservoir, where the water is cooler. "If you were on fish along a channel dropoff in 20 feet of water, then can't locate them on your next outing, don't panic — start trolling the heavy sinker rig upriver, following the channel until you get back on fish," the guide advised.

Morgan targets flowing tributaries in hot weather. "Crappie in the lower end of the reservoir will often move to the nearest flowing creek rather than follow the old river channel upstream. A flowing creek is cooler and more highly oxygenated than the rest of the lake in summer, so use your boat's surface temperature gauge to locate the coolest tributaries."

Spring holes are also dynamite late-summer crappie spots, Morgan said. "These are places where underground springs enter the lake; spring water is a constant, cool temperature year-'round; in summer, the area close to the spring will be significantly cooler than elsewhere in the lake. Spring holes are commonly located in tributaries with a limestone bottom and may be indicated on a good topo map."

Harold also finds old farm ponds to be great late-summer crappie attractors. "Farmland that was inundated when the reservoir was formed may have multiple stock ponds. These are often loaded with brush, drawing large schools of crappie."

MORE HOT STUFF FROM HAROLD

- A GPS unit is a useful tool when crappie are on their deep summer pattern. Note coordinates in a logbook and make a milk run from spot to spot.

- In snaggy areas, replace the heavy bell sinker with a slender homemade sinker fashioned out of a section of brass or steel rod. Welding rod with a diameter of 5/32 inch works great — an 8-inch length weighs approximately 3/4 ounce. Drill a small hole in one end for your line; sand this smooth before use.

- Other gamefish besides crappie inhabit the deep channel structures discussed in this article. You're likely to catch bass, hybrids, even stripers while using this technique, so avoid ultralight tackle, and keep your drag loose.

- Deep trolling and vertical fishing are cover-intensive techniques, and line abrasion is common when using them. Check frequently for rough spots in your line and retie often.

- Don't be alarmed at high water temperatures. Crappie will bite actively even when the surface temperature approaches 100 degrees!

- Drink plenty of water, wear a hat and use sunscreen on summer outings.

HOW HAROLD KEEPS HIS MINNOWS FRISKY IN HOT WEATHER

Live crappie minnows demand special care in hot weather.

Harold Morgan finds a Styrofoam bucket stays much cooler than a metal bucket. He replaces the Styrofoam top with a heavier top made from a circular piece of wood; this won't blow off when running between fishing spots at high speeds. An inexpensive battery-powered aerator, available at most discount stores, provides ample oxygen to Morgan's minnows and is much gentler than a boat's livewell aerator. He recommends using a bait-saver chemical to condition bait bucket water. "Don't add ice to your bucket; minnows swimming in cold water will go into shock when you put them in hot lake water. The water in your bucket will stay cooler if you avoid sticking your hands in it; use a dip net to catch bait instead. After each fishing trip, scrub your bucket out thoroughly with liquid detergent, then rinse."

Lively minnows make all the difference!

FISH CURRENT FOR SUMMER SLABS

Ever notice that crappie fishing seems to grind to a halt during mid-summer? It's not just your imagination — there are verifiable reasons why the dreaded "dog days" can indeed spell poor fishing. Many lakes suffer oxygen depletion in summer, which causes crappie to become lethargic and, in extreme cases, can lead to fish kills. Some Sun Belt lakes may have surface temperatures approaching 100 degrees, putting crappie into a stupor or sending them into the depths where they're hard to locate and catch.

Fortunately, not every body of water containing crappie is subject to the summer doldrums. Great fishing is typically found on river-run reservoirs, those man-made lakes where current flow is regulated by an upstream dam. As you're about to learn, current breathes life into the ecosystem and can be responsible for a tremendous crappie bite...*if* you know how to fish it properly. Here, Steve McCadams and Jim Duckworth explain how they use current to their advantage when targeting summer slabs. Their insights into this seldom-discussed topic can turn those dog days into the most exciting crappie fishing season of the year.

WIRTH: You seldom hear anglers who fish for anything but trout or catfish say anything good about current. To the contrary, most fishermen find it a nuisance. What can current mean to the serious crappie fisherman?

McCADAMS: Current has a rejuvenating effect on a reservoir that's especially noticeable in summer. When there's generation from the upstream dam, fresh, cool water washes down through the system. This helps keep the summer temperature of a river-run reservoir significantly cooler than that of a slack-water lake. Plus, the tumbling action of current distributes significant amounts of dissolved oxygen throughout the entire water column — slack-water lakes, on the other hand, are often low in oxygen in hot weather below a certain depth. You also don't get the stratification or "layering" of hot or oxygen-depleted water in a river-run reservoir that you get in lakes with no current. Current also jump-starts the food chain. It stirs up plankton and algae, which stimulates shad and other baitfish to move around and start feeding. Gamefish higher up the food chain, including crappie, sense an increase in forage activity and become more active as well.

DUCKWORTH: Current also positions crappie in predictable places. They'll face upstream in current to feed on minnows that are moving in the direction of the flow. If you know the dam's generation schedule, you can get a good idea of when the best feeding times will be. As Steve indicated, crappie in a river-run environment tend to feed when there's some current moving, because they instinctively know their forage will be most active then.

WIRTH: Do crappie favor light, moderate or heavy current?

McCADAMS: I find they use current as a food-delivery system, but will do what they can to get out of anything greater than a light flow. If there's light generation, they'll hold right in the current, but when it picks up, they'll move behind objects on the bottom such as rocks, trees, stumps, etc. The water is then flowing over and past them at a good clip, but they're sitting in slack water behind a current break. From this vantage point, they can hold for long periods regardless of the flow, and rush out to grab a passing meal.

DUCKWORTH: It's important to understand that current isn't the same throughout the entire water column — it tends to be slower on the surface and bottom than in the middle, due to air and bottom friction. Even during a fairly strong flow, irregularities of the bottom contour may slow down the current enough to make it comfortable for crappie.

WIRTH: Besides sitting on the bottom behind objects, where else do crappie gravitate during current generation?

McCADAMS: They love eddies – a lot of food concentrates in these areas. They'll also get on the down-current side of a ledge or sand bar, especially if there's some stumps, rocks or brush there.

DUCKWORTH: I also catch 'em on the back sides of humps and islands – any place trash collects, they'll be there.

WIRTH: Do you normally catch bigger crappie from river-run reservoirs than slack-water impoundments, and if so, why?

McCADAMS: Definitely! Crappie don't have to move around nearly as much when they have current as a food delivery system. They learn to go into a holding pattern when there's no current running and wait until it cranks up again to feed. They get big, fat and lazy when current brings the food to them.

DUCKWORTH: I actually catch bigger crappie in deep, clear highland reservoirs with no current flow like Tennessee's Center Hill and Dale Hollow lakes, but crappie are far less numerous in these bodies of water than in murky river-run reservoirs. The average size, however, tends to be excellent in current reservoirs.

WIRTH: How do crappie react to intermittent current generation?

McCADAMS: Generation is often heaviest in a river-run reservoir in summer, when power demands are highest – it takes lots of juice to keep all those air conditioners running. I find the feeding times of crappie are strongly tied to water movement, and in summer, the same generation schedule often prevails for long periods. The bite tends to be strongest during the first hour or so of generation, probably because of all the plankton that's uprooted during this period. Then after an hour or so, the bite usually stabilizes. If generation kicks in by mid-morning for several days running, the fish will get strongly acclimated to this, and the bite will be predictably good around 10 o'clock or so. They will usually stay on a mid-morning feeding pattern until he schedule changes.

DUCKWORTH: The bite is usually strongest while the current is running, but crappie bite better than either most other species in the lake, including bass or stripers, when the current shuts down. You just have to fish differently for them. When generation stops, they move off the bottom and away from cover, and suspend in the water column, usually just above the thermocline. I'll often vertical-jig these fish 20 to 25 feet deep.

McCADAMS: Crappie are a lot more scattered out than when current is running, and usually on deeper structures – 18 to 25 feet would be a good average depth. Trolling with multiple pole rigs is a good option now. You want to use a shotgun approach instead of a rifle approach, because the fish won't be holding tight to current breaks and eddies.

WIRTH: So when current flows, crappie tend to move shallower on structure?

McCADAMS: Right, but remember it's summer, so they won't move *too* shallow. If they were 25 feet deep with no generation, they might slide up to 15 feet, but not 5. The baitfish will dictate where and how shallow they move, so always watch your graph for schools of shad and concentrate your efforts at that level.

DUCKWORTH: I've caught 'em extremely shallow in weedbeds adjacent to a flowing channel. A ton of bait can pack into the grass now, and crappie will move in to gorge themselves. Then when the current stops, the bait scatters and the crappie go deeper.

WIRTH: Clarify why baitfish move when current starts flowing.

DUCKWORTH: Many crappie anglers believe the current literally washes the baitfish into an area, just as they believe the wind blows the bait around. Actually, healthy baitfish have little problem dealing with either current or wind. They move because their food source, plankton and algae, are subject to the whims of current.

McCADAMS: True, but out of a big school of shad, you're going to have many sick or injured individuals, and they represent a huge feeding opportunity for crappie. These less healthy baitfish are swept away when current kicks in, and crappie waiting downstream suck 'em up like a vacuum cleaner.

WIRTH: We've touched on bait and lure presentations in current, but let's get into this subject deeper. What presentation techniques work best when the water is moving?

McCADAMS: I prefer a vertical presentation with a bottom-bumping "Kentucky" rig with multiple hooks. It's critical when current is flowing to use enough weight on the end of your line so you can stay in touch with both the bottom and cover – I generally use a 1-ounce bell sinker in a light to moderate flow. I tie two hooks 18 inches apart and bait up with live minnows. By slowly dragging and bumping the sinker along the bottom, I'm presenting baits at two different levels in the water column. Very often most of my bites will come on either the lower or higher of the two hooks. This tells me the fish are either holding around the base of the cover, a common scenario when there's a pretty good flow, or suspended right above the cover, which is typical during light generation. I also keep several rods rigged up with different line diameters. Normally I use 14 to 17 pound test on the Kentucky rig in light current, but I'll switch to 12 pound in faster current.

DUCKWORTH: I fish a lot of artificials in moving water. My favorite is the Slider Whirly Bee grub spinner. I'll cast it upstream and retrieve it close to the bottom with a series of light jerks – this is a fantastic presentation on river bars with brush on the ends. I'll also use a marabou jig set 2 to 4 feet under a bobber and cast into eddies — the jig suspends and shakes with the motion of the swirling current. I generally stick to 6 pound line when fishing current, because there's less line drag, and so I can break off easily when I get hung up. In murky water, I'll slow-troll small crankbaits, keeping them just off bottom.

WIRTH: Summing up, what's your final advice to crappie anglers about fishing current?

McCADAMS: Have several rods pre-rigged so you can get another presentation out there quickly when you get hung up – it you've only got one rod, by the time you re-tie, you may have drifted 200 yards from your spot. Use your graph and a set of marker buoys to pinpoint offshore ledges and humps that hold baitfish and crappie when current is being generated.

DUCKWORTH: Get a trolling motor that's more powerful than you think you'll ever need – it'll hold your boat in position when they switch on the current. Keep everything you're going to need – tacklebox, pliers, water jug – close by so you don't have to root around in storage boxes looking for them while your boat drifts off crappie-holding structure. And always wear your life jacket.

DEALING-WITH CURRENT

Current energizes and positions crappie in summer, and can lead to a fantastic crappie bite. But it can also be frustrating to fish. Here are some tips from top crappie guides for dealing with moving water.

- Current creates drag on heavy lines, causing presentations to miss their mark. As a rule of thumb, reduce line diameter from 1/3 to 1/2 when current is flowing.

- Keep a utility box equipped with jig heads and sinkers of various weights and go heavier or lighter as current dictates.

- In light to moderate current, position the bow of your boat upstream when working a large piece of structure such as a ledge or river bar, and use your trolling motor to hold your position or adjust your position.

- Anchoring can be the most effective way to fish channel-related structures such as dropoffs when significant current is flowing. "River rats" know you'll need 3 feet of anchor rope for every foot of water you're anchoring in, and 1 pound of anchor for every foot of boat length – using less than this formula will make it difficult or impossible for the anchor to bite and hold.

- To fish a mid-stream structure such as a hump or ledge, drop anchor on the upstream side of the structure and let out enough rope so the boat can drift downstream past the target. Once the anchor bites, let out additional rope or shorten the rope length (using your outboard or trolling motor to move upstream if necessary) as needed.

WHAT TO DO WHEN THE CURRENT SHUTS OFF

Crappie in river-run reservoirs are geared to feeding during periods of current generation. However, you can still catch fish when generation stops.

On-again, off-again current is a fact of life on river-run impoundments. As a rule of thumb, crappie hold tighter to cover when current is running, then move out of cover and suspend once generation stops. Sometimes it's hard to tell whether the water is slack or moving, so look at the channel buoys to see if current is swirling around them and plan your presentation accordingly.

When current has halted, Garry Mason, famous for his lure casting approach, switches to a modified Kentucky rig: a single Slider grub with a Berkley Power Niblet impaled on the hook rigged 18 inches to 2 feet up the line. Main-lake dropoffs are his #1 summer crappie structures; he uses marker buoys to delineate channel drops and river ledges, and always keeps an eye out for baitfish schools. "Crappie generally drop deeper once generation stops – if they were at 12 feet in current, 18 feet is a likely depth during no-flow periods," he says. "They'll be suspended up from the bottom or over brushy cover, and will usually be scattered out along the drop, rather than bunched up in a small area. Once you've set out your markers, use your trolling motor to move slowly along the structure, alternately tapping the sinker on bottom and reeling the rig straight when through baitfish schools suspended higher in the water column when you spot them on your graph."

Fishing out in the middle of the lake in midsummer can be taxing even for a hard-core angler Mason. He carries a patio umbrella in his boat for shade and brings along plenty of water and sunscreen.

Not all crappie move deep in midsummer. Here's how Harold Morgan catches 'em up shallow during the so-called "dog days."

SHALLOW SUMMER CRAPPIE

How hot was it?

Insufferably hot. August-in-Tennessee hot. Fry-eggs-on-the-pavement hot. But not too hot to be catching crappie!

Here it was, the middle of the day with the air temperature right at 100 degrees, yet Harold Morgan's livewell was chock full of slabs. And we hadn't even left the tributary arm where he launched his boat! At the mouth of the creek, jet skis buzzed like swarming gnats. "Most crappie fishermen hate hot weather," the guide laughed as he reeled in another fish. "I don't know about you, but I can stand a little heat when the fishing's this fast." Just then a ski boat idled past us, and a bikini-clad blonde smiled and waved as Harold held up the crappie. "Besides," he laughed, "you can't complain about the scenery!"

In the mythology of crappie fishing, summertime brings on the dreaded Dog Days, a torturous time when heat and humidity soar and fish lips clamp tightly shut. To the hapless angler, a day on the water now seems like a sentence to hell, with not even an occasional tug on the line to distract him from the sweltering, dripping, unrelenting heat.

But count on Morgan to have aces up his sleeve whenever conditions threaten to slow down the crappie bite. "If you play your cards right, you can score some nice fish in short order in midsummer, and you don't have to fish deep to catch 'em," he'd promised me before we set out on this hot-weather crappie excursion. As usual, he was right on the money.

PIECE OF THE PUZZLE

"There was a time when I hesitated to even talk about catching crappie in midsummer *period,* let alone from shallow water," Morgan explained. "Whenever I'd tell folks I was slammin' lots of good fish up shallow from June through September, they'd look at me like I was either crazy or lying. I remember mentioning a great July crappie trip to one of my long-time customers when I ran into him at the dock. He laughed and said, "Harold, I didn't fall off the pumpkin truck. Don't feed me that baloney!' After that, I didn't talk about my shallow summer patterns for years."

But today's crappie fishermen are better-skilled and more open-minded than in the past, Morgan added. "There's greater interest in, and awareness of, the seasonal movements of crappie now than before, thanks in large part to the education anglers have received from this magazine," he said. "The skilled crappie angler now understands that once crappie leave their spring spawning grounds, they don't evaporate into thin air, but rather migrate into areas that suit their needs as the seasons progress. And the shallow summer pattern is a natural part of these seasonal movements, just another piece of the crappie fishing puzzle."

Quest for Knowledge

Morgan is quick to add that he's still learning about shallow summer patterns. "I pick up more tidbits of information every day I fish in summer," he explained. "Some of the things I've discovered lately will surely turn the heads of long-time crappie addicts."

Anyone who's fished for crappie as long as Harold Morgan has, is bound to have plenty of preconceived notions about the haunts and habits of these gamefish, But you'd do well to put these ideas on the shelf once summer rolls around, he insisted. "Like any veteran crappie angler, I have my own way of doing things. I used to figure all the crappie were out in deep water once June arrived and the lake's surface temperature hit the low 80s. For years, my sole summer pattern was to fish isolated stumps, brushpiles and stake beds on creek and river channel dropoffs, deep main-lake flats, long points with a slow taper into deep water, and offshore humps. Here crappie had more current flow from the main river channel and tributary channels, which meant greater levels of dissolved oxygen and plentiful bait. Invariably the fish were deep on this pattern; I found the 17 to 23 foot zone consistently productive for large schools of quality crappie."

But Morgan's quest for total understanding of the crappie's summer movements eventually led him into uncharted territory, including shallow bays, coves and tributary arms. "I often had my afternoons free during the summer months, since most of my guide trips during this period ran from dawn 'til noon due to the heat," he continued.

"So once my clients left, I'd nose around shallow areas during the hottest part of the day, and I was astounded at what I found."

One thing Harold quickly discovered: water can't get too hot for crappie. "I've found they'll bite shallow regardless of the surface temperature. I've personally caught 'em in 95-degree water, and I know fishermen down in Mississippi who load the boat all summer long in their shallow lakes, even when the surface temp tops 100 degrees."

Shallow Summer Scenarios

Morgan has learned that there are certain scenarios where crappie will move shallow in summer, and when these opportunities present themselves, you can score some unbelievable catches. He listed the following as prime examples:

Trees on dropoffs and sloping banks – "I call these 'elevator trees' because crappie use 'em to move up and down in the water column," he explained. "Typically the best summer laydown trees have their trunks resting on shore or in shallow water adjacent to a sloping bank, with their branches fanning out across a deep channel, ditch or other major dropoff. The perfect tree has the ends of its longest branches sticking out like extended fingers into deep, open water. The trunk and branches develop a coating of algae, which baitfish feed upon. Crappie schools moving along the channel will encounter the tree and follow the branches and trunk into shallower water to feed. In clear lakes, they'll often position themselves around the 10-foot zone around the tree; they may be only a couple feet deep if the water is murky."

A lone tree may pull in a huge number of crappie from a wide area, Morgan said. "If you don't see any fish on your graph in the 15 to 25 foot zone on open-water structures, move to the nearest fallen tree – betcha you'll load the boat!"

Harold loves to fish fallen trees with a twist-tail grub or small tube jug. He'll move out to the end of the tree and cast parallel to the trunk. "Start by targeting the shady side of the tree. Let the jig fall until the line goes slack, then instantly turn the reel handle at a slow to moderate pace, swimming the lure down the trunk toward deeper water. If you feel it tick the wood, speed up slightly. Don't hop-and-drop the bait — you'll hang up for sure."

Windy days – "Most crappie fishermen try to avoid the wind, but if there's ever a time to fish in a windy spot, it's in midsummer," Morgan insisted. "A stiff breeze will push drifting plankton blooms from the main lake into the shallows, bringing big schools of shad along with it. Crappie are more interested in an easy meal than staying deep, and they'll pull of stakes and follow their forage shallow in a heartbeat. So when you're out there on those deep humps and ledges and the wind starts knockin' you around, move to the nearest wind-blown shallow area for some fast action."

Compared to the fallen tree scenario mentioned above, this is an open-water pattern, one where the crappie are likely to be suspended. Morgan drift-trolls a combination of tube and twister jigs and live minnows weighted down with split shot behind his boat, criss-crossing a shallow bay or tributary cove. "I start about 12 feet deep around a long point or flat and work progressively shallower, alternatively following a depth contour and then cutting across several contours in a lazy S pattern," he said. "Often the fish are loosely scattered on this pattern, so you'll pick 'em up at various depths."

Don't be surprised if something considerably larger than a crappie makes a run with your lure or bait, Harold added: "Besides crappie,

I've caught big largemouth and smallmouth bass, hybrids and stripers on this pattern."

Low dissolved oxygen – "On some Sun Belt lakes, dissolved oxygen levels may become extremely low in midsummer," Morgan noted. "Following an extended period of cloudy weather, plankton, which depends on sunlight for survival, often dies and drifts toward the bottom, where it decays – this phenomenon is known as 'fallout' by biologists. The decay process burns up oxygen, and water below the 8 to 10 foot zone may become dangerously low in dissolved oxygen, forcing baitfish and gamefish shallower."

Unlike the first two patterns mentioned, this one most commonly occurs in open water. "I don't own a dissolved oxygen meter, but I can always tell this pattern has kicked in when I see bait and crappie schools on my graph suspended high in the water column over deep main-lake structures," Morgan indicated. "I vertical-fish these deep spots with a Kentucky rig, which has a heavy bell sinker at the end of the line and live minnows or jigs on short leader lines above the sinker. When I'm not catching any crappie while bumping the sinker along the bottom, I'll reel up to move to another spot, and might catch two crappie at once when the rig enters the 10 foot zone right under my boat. This happened so often at Priest Lake near Nashville that I asked a fisheries biologist about it; he said the lake was suffering from low oxygen levels. So the moral of the story is, if you aren't catching 'em near the bottom on deep structure in summer, reel straight up and you might locate a big school of fish."

Inflowing murky water — "Often in summer, heat and humidity cause a buildup of thundershowers," Harold said. "These summer storms can be real toad-stranglers, sending a great deal of muddy water into the system via the tributaries. This murky runoff is a veritable chowder of insects, worms and microscopic organisms, and calls in minnows like a dinner bell. Crappie that were in deeper water sense the feeding opportunity and move into the murky runoff for an easy meal."

After heading for the back of a tributary arm, Morgan casts a chartreuse grub, twister or small crankbait into the murky inflow. "I've caught slab crappie as shallow as 1 foot on this pattern," he claimed. "There can be an unbelievable number of fish ganged up in that shallow runoff to put on the feed bag."

TARGET CURRENT EDGES FOR SHALLOW SUMMER CRAPPIE

Harold Morgan knows that big summer crappie thrive around moving water. "Slack-water lakes tend to develop a deep thermocline in summer, which may position baitfish and crappie below 30 feet. But rivers and river-run reservoirs with marked current flow stay cooler in midsummer and have a more consistent temperature from top to bottom, without marked stratification. In this environment, there's really no reason for crappie to be deep. You can often score major-league catches in 8 feet of water or less. Crappie don't usually stay in current, but prefer to gravitate to edges where slack and moving water meet. Here they find it easy to suspend for long periods and wait for baitfish schools to pass by in the current. Fish this pattern by keying on long points and large main-lake flats with scattered wood cover during periods of current generation. On cloudy days, fan-cast a grub or tube bait around the structures, targeting water less than 10 feet deep with a slow swimming retrieve for loosely-scattered fish. On sunny days, crappie will hold tighter to stumps and brushpiles;

cast the same lures to shallow stumps, often scoring an immediate strike when the bait knocks on wood."

OPEN-WATER TACTICS FOR SUMMER CRAPPIE

If you're like most crappie fisherman, chances are you hang up your rods and poles after the spring bedding season is over. After all, once the water heats up and the fish move out of the shallows, there's not much hope of finding and catching crappie...right?

Wrong! Summer can be a fantastic time of year to catch crappie, so long as you abandon your preconceived notions about this great gamefish and your usual methods of catching it.

JIM DUCKWORTH'S SUMMER STRATEGIES

Jim Duckworth is a master at deciphering the subtleties of both moving- and slackwater reservoirs. He believes crappie anglers are missing the boat big-time by not fishing during the summer months. "The fish run big and stack up in incredible numbers. Plus, the fishing is very consistent. No cold fronts to deal with, little rising or falling water — I have some my best crappie action of the year in hot weather."

Sizzling summer water temperatures are the rule on the waters where Duckworth guides. "Surface temperatures are routinely between 90 and 95 degrees; this pushes the fish to the edge of the thermocline," he said. "It's critical to know where this cooler band of water is on your home waters." According to Jim, the easiest way to find the thermocline is to take your graph off the "auto" mode and put it on "manual," then crank up the sensitivity until a band appears across the screen. "Often you'll see baitfish and gamefish, including crappie, suspending right at or just above this level," Duckworth explained. "Generally crappie find the area just above the thermocline to have the most favorable temperature range. The water below the thermocline is usually too low in dissolved oxygen to support large numbers of crappie."

Summer crappie require a persistent approach. "They won't move around much to chase down a meal — on some days, they can be downright lethargic. But you can catch 'em in by repeatedly presenting a lure or live bait right in their faces. The tradeoff to their lack of aggressiveness in hot water is that there are often large numbers of crappie stacked close together, and many of them are good-sized."

We've all heard about crappie "stacking up;" this is literally the case during the summer season, Jim indicated. "They'll often form a tower that may cover a 25-foot band of water. I try to aim my presentation at the middle of this tower, which is where I usually find the most catchable fish. For some reason fish at the top and bottom of the tower seem to be the toughest to catch."

It's paramount to locate several schools of crappie, then test-fish each school until you find one with some active fish, Duckworth said. "Sometimes I'll fish 10 or 15 schools until I get on one where the fish will cooperate. I don't like to stay on an inactive school too long, 'cause I feel if I keep moving, I'll eventually find one that'll have some good fish that are willing to bite." Surprisingly, Jim isn't a slave to locating large concentrations of baitfish in hot weather: "Summer crappie feed only sporadically, so I don't worry about whether or not there's a big supply of bait in the area."

During summer, Duckworth looks for crappie in the following locations:

- *Bridges* — "They provide open-water shade, so the water is cooler. There's usually some current flow around a bridge, meaning higher levels of dissolved oxygen.

- *Standing timber* — "I especially like timber lining the old river channel. Again, the water will be cooler and more highly-oxygenated here."

- *Deep brushy points* — "Most crappie fishermen sink brushpiles in shallow tributary arms, but every year I make it a point to sink some brush on points tapering into 20 to 35 feet of water, specifically for summer fishing."

- *Channel bends* — "Most of these will be out on the make river channel. Sometimes cover in the form of limbs or entire trees will wash into the deeper bends during spring floods, providing a perfect haven for summer crappie."

- *Deep humps* — "A main-lake hump will pull in a tremendous number of crappie from a wide area. The best humps have stumps or brush on them. Crappie tend to suspend over these structures at their comfort level."

Duckworth relies on two types of presentations in hot weather:

- *Trolling tactics* — "Summer is an ideal time to troll for open-water crappie, and the most efficient way to cover a lot of water. The #5 Rapala Shad Rap, the Heddon Wally Diver (a walleye lure), Rebel's Deep Wee R, the Series 200 and 200 Bandit, and Storm's Hot-N-Tot in shad patterns are all excellent trolling lures. These lures run around 12 to 15 feet deep on 8 pound mono, which usually isn't deep enough — remember, the most catchable fish may be 30 feet deep. I usually fix a Carolina-type rig for trolling, with a half-ounce sinker on my main line, followed by a bead (to protect the knot), swivel and a 2- to 3-foot leader line. You can also use lead-core line with a mono leader, or a drop sinker like Gapen's Bait Walker, to get your crankbait down. Run multiple rods, each with the lure running at a different depth, until you determine where the fish are biting best."

- *Crappie jigs* — "Small tube or twister jigs fished vertically will also produce. Even though I'm fishing deep, I like the lightest jig I can get away with, 'cause summer crappie can be very reluctant to bite and may immediately reject an offering that doesn't feel 100% natural. I either add a tiny tuffy minnow to the jig hook or dip the lure in a baitfish-flavored attractant."

TAKE THE FAST LANE TO SUMMER SLABS

For sure-fire summer crappie action, fish submerged roadbeds. "These are dynamite places for crappie to stack up in hot water," says Duckworth. "They'll sit on a good road all summer long, with more and more fish joining the school until there's a huge tower of crappie over the structure."

OPEN-WATER TACTICS FOR SUMMER CRAPPIE

The best roadbeds have some sort of irregular cover lining either side: a submerged bridge, either intact or in pieces; stumps; broken-up pieces of concrete, brushpiles, etc. "Roadbeds are good crappie attractors by themselves, but a little cover is like gravy — it makes 'em even better." Roadbeds are easy structures to locate — most reservoirs have several old roads entering the water. In summer, crappie will be shallower (10-15 feet) on these structures if the water is murky; deeper (up to 30 feet) if the water is clear. Use your graph and a set of marker buoys to pinpoint the location of the road as it extends out into the lake, then vertical-jig, drift or troll the structure, using the tips you've just read.

Jim Duckworth trolled up this fine crappie near a baitfish school in open water.

When fall arrives, most anglers put up their crappie gear. But that's when Kentucky Lake guide Tom Moody enjoys some of the best fishing of the year.

LATE-SEASON TIPS FOR SUPERSLABS

Last weekend saw autumn at its peak, with the trees on the shores of your local lake a riot of red, yellow and orange. Then a major cold front blew in, and the accompanying wind and rain took their toll, leaving behind bare branches, a chill in the air and the certainty that winter is just around the corner.

If you're like most crappie anglers, you're probably thinking it's time to drydock your boat and hang up your poles. But before you do, take time to read what follows.

Fish Deep Dropoffs

"Once the lake chills down in late fall, large numbers of crappie pull out to the deeper dropoffs and suspend," says Tom Moody. "Now is the time to move offshore and hunt for a well-defined creek or river channel drop – one that makes a rapid descent from around 10 to 12 feet to at least 18 feet. You'll find large schools of quality fish schooled up on these drops, usually adjacent to sunken brushpiles, trees or stake beds."

Moody uses the popular Kentucky rig to score limit catches when crappie are on this deep pattern. The leader hooks are baited with medium-size shiners – don't use bait that's too small this time of year, he says. Tom fishes the rig on a light-action spinning rod with 8 to 10 pound line.

Moody idles along the dropoff, tossing out several marker buoys to delineate the structure. He then and moves slowly along the drop with his electric motor, probing the structure with the Kentucky rig as he goes. "This time of year I always free-line the rig all the way to the bottom, then reel up approximately three turns of the reel handle," he explained. "This puts the lower minnow about 2 feet off bottom, which is a common depth for suspending fish. I pay attention to whether my first couple of fish are caught on the upper or lower hook, then adjust my presentation accordingly. The fish tend to pack tightly together now, and zeroing in on their precise depth is important – a miss is as good as a mile."

Moody says a crisp 45-degree day with a light breeze out of the south is optimal for this late-season pattern. "Some wind is desirable, because it allows you to use your electric motor sparingly for a more stealthy presentation," he noted. "High winds mean increased wave action, which can cause the water to turn murky. This will usually result in a much slower bite, so move to another area of the lake where the water isn't so rough and roiled."

Target Schools of Small Minnows

"In late fall and winter, size matters when it comes to minnows," believes Jim Duckworth. "Once the water temp drops below 60 degrees, crappie may bypass larger baitfish in favor of immature shad and shiners. These are from the last spawn of the year, and are usually around an inch in length. There are billions of 'em in most reservoirs by mid-November, and they're a primary food source for crappie."

Duckworth finds clouds of these itty-bitty baitfish suspended in the middle of tributary arms, often between 10 and 14 feet deep. Schools of crappie are seldom far away. "This is an open-water pattern, and trolling crankbaits is the most effective way to exploit it," he advised. "I'll troll 200-series Bandit crankbaits in reflective shad patterns at 2 mph with my trolling motor or gas outboard, making multiple passes through a good school of crappie. I'll often pick up two or three fish on every pass."

The guide also trolls creek channel drops, tributary flats with a deep-water access and creek channels with stumps along their edges, again looking for schools of tiny baitfish. "The biggest mistake you can make now is using a lure than runs too deep," he cautioned. "The 200-series Bandit runs 10 feet deep on 8 pound mono; in a clear lake, it'll pull crappie up from as deep as 25 feet."

Don't Overlook Shallow Water

"Surprisingly, many crappie may refuse to move deep late in the year," says Harold Morgan. "I routinely catch them from 2 to 4 feet deep when the lake temperature is in the mid to upper 50s, a time when most crappie anglers are fishing deep."

Morgan said the key to scoring major-league catches on his shallow pattern is waiting until late afternoon to fish it. "The fish often suspend in deeper water, waiting for the sun to warm up the shallows a degree or two before they move up," he explained. "I've had some of my best early-winter catches between 3 and 4:30 in the afternoon, after most of the other fishermen on the lake have gone home."

Twisters and tubes rigged on lightweight jigheads will provide plenty of action now, Harold promised. "Make a long cast past any shallow submerged wood cover you can locate, then swim the lure back to the boat with a slow, steady retrieve. Don't hop, skip or jump the jig, just reel it straight in. These fish may be shallow, but that doesn't mean they're aggressive — their metabolism is slow in that cold water, and they're unlikely to chase down a fast-moving bait."

Harold says it's important to experiment with color when crappie are sluggish. "Sometimes you can provoke a reaction strike with a hot-colored bait. If you aren't getting hits on white or green, try red, pink or chartreuse."

Fish Remaining Grass

"Most fishermen know that bass, pike and muskies relate to submerged grassbeds, but are surprised to learn that in certain lakes, crappie will hang around weeds as well," claims Fred McClintock. His home lake, 27,000-acre Dale Hollow Reservoir, has little submerged wood cover, but sports lush beds of coontail and milfoil growing down to 30 feet; it's here that the guide scores impressive crappie catches in early winter. "Crappie cover is a relative term," Fred pointed out. "These fish will use whatever cover they can find, and in a rocky lake like Dale Hollow that has few submerged stumps and brushpiles, they won't hesitate to gravitate to grass."

McClintock locates deep grassbeds on his graph, and notes the depth of "hooks" indicating crappie suspending over the cover. He then drift-trolls 1/8- to 1/4-ounce tube or twister jigs on 6 pound mono, using his electric motor to control boat speed and position. Proximity to deep water makes the grass more attractive to crappie now, Fred has found. "This pattern is strongest in early December, when the weeds in 10 feet of water or less are starting to die off," he said. "The deeper weeds remain alive, giving off oxygen and attracting baitfish, and will draw crappie from a wide area."

Keep a light drag when fishing this pattern, McClintock added. " Last winter, besides catching a ton of slab crappie, we caught a 6-pound smallmouth bass and an 18-pound muskie while drifting jigs over deep weeds."

Target Channel Bends

The path to great late-season crappie action can be a crooked one, says Garry Mason. Like some of the other experts we interviewed, Mason keys on dropoffs once autumn transitions into winter, but he invariably catches his biggest fish were the channel makes a sharp bend. "A channel bend is a tremendous crappie concentrator," he remarked. "You may fish a straight creek channel ledge for hours and pick up a few scattered fish, then load the boat where the channel makes a sharp turn. If there's some brush or stumps on top of the drop, so much the better. Crappie will gang up in huge numbers on these spots."

Mason motors halfway back into a tributary arm, then follows the channel out into the main lake with his graph. "Late in the year, I'll start by checking the 8 to 10 foot ledge on top of the drop, then move out over the channel itself, then back on top of the ledge, in a lazy S pattern. I spend a good deal of time looking for the right combination of channel bends, cover and baitfish, because I know once I'm on the right spot, the bite will be awesome."

Mason drops a marker buoy on a productive channel bend and fishes the spot thoroughly, targeting several different depths. " I use a Kentucky rig with jigheads baited with small minnows late, and will add a Berkley Power Bait Crappie Niblet to the hook as an attractor – these help activate a stronger bite when crappie are a bit sluggish," he said. "I'll drop the rig to the bottom, then s-l-o-w-l-y reel it straight up until I contact fish. Sometimes the fish closest to bottom will be most active; sometimes the shallower fish will bite best."

If you don't see crappie on your graph the first time you check out a channel bend, revisit the spot later in the day, Mason suggested. "Often crappie moving along the dropoff will use the bend as a rest stop. The more fish that congregate here, the better your chances of limiting out, for crappie are highly competitive feeders."

Fish Big-Bays & Flats

"Most late-season anglers move out to fast-sloping main lake structures for a crappie fix," Steve McCadams has found. "I like to fish bays and flats instead. These are fairly shallow structures with a gradual slope, not the kinds of spots you'd normally think of as a fall/winter transitional crappie haunt. But believe me, they can hold plenty of fish."

These often-overlooked structures hold mega-quantities of bait, the guide knows. "Once the lake temp has dropped into the 50s, threadfin shad pack into reservoir bays and flats in unbelievable numbers, and crappie head there to put on the feed bag before winter sends them packing for deep water. This is the most consistent, predictable reservoir crappie pattern I've seen during this time of year, and I'm amazed more people aren't fishing it."

Steve targets wood cover in the 6 to 12 foot zone on these mid-depth spots. He'll use a variety of presentations, from vertical-jigging tube baits to slow-trolling spider rigs. "If you find wood, you'll catch fish," he promised. "Crappie may suspend a great deal in summer and early fall, but once the water chills, they like to stick tight to cover."

BLUFFS HOLD BIG-FISH

Donny Hall knows that river and creek channel bluffs are strong magnets for superslabs in late fall. "Crappie transitioning from shallow tributary arms to deep main lake structures use steep rock bluffs like highways," he said. "Besides serving as migration routes, these structures offer forage and cover opportunities that crappie can't pass up."

Rock bluffs develop a slick coating of algae which shad feed upon, Hall indicated: "You'll see huge schools of baitfish swimming right along the bluff, and where there's lots of bait, big crappie aren't far behind. In addition, the base of the bluff is typically littered with rocks of various sizes that have broken off the rocky face, providing great hiding places for crappie. Over the years, I've caught some of my biggest slabs from these structures."

Hall's favorite bluff pattern is trolling 1/8 ounce lipless vibrating crankbaits along ledges that jut out from the base of the bluff. "The best crappie bluffs aren't straight up and down, but have a series of ledges that stairstep from shallow to deep water," he explained. "In late fall, crappie often gang up on 15- to 20-foot ledges, where they sit and wait for baitfish schools to pass by. Troll a small Rat-L-Trap along this ledge on 8 pound line, moving just fast enough to make the lure vibrate – I guarantee you'll catch fish."

SCORE MONSTER CRAPPIE DURING FALL DRAWDOWN

Most flood-control reservoirs undergo a major drawdown every fall. The lake level is lowered in anticipation of heavy spring rains, and this can impact crappie location and mood. Here are some tips for scoring more and bigger crappie when they pull the plug on your local waters:

- "During drawdown, many crappie will pull out of the shallows and move to main-lake bars and ledges," McCadams indicated. "They evidently feel more secure in or close to deep water. I catch many fish on 14 to 18 foot bars while drawdown is taking place; they may move shallower once the lake level stabilizes."

- "Pay attention to changing lake levels, for crappie definitely orient to deeper water during drawdown," Hall has found. "The move can take place overnight. If you were catching fish in 4 feet of water around brushpiles on Saturday, then notice the lake level has dropped several inches when you come back on Sunday, back off to the first 10-foot water you can find that has wood cover. You may have to use a slower, more patient presentation during drawdown – it sometimes disorients the fish."

- "The juncture of a tributary mouth and the main river cannel is a key spot during drawdown," advised Duckworth. "Position your boat on the downstream side of creek channel brushpiles – crappie will position themselves behind this cover — and swim a grub slowly through it. If you feel the lure hang up, pop the rod tip gently and it'll usually come through."

WINTER CRAPPIE PATTERNS

Winter's an awesome time to fish crappie in the Sun Belt. No iceover — that's a given. Fishing pressure is usually super-light, since many outdoorsmen here hang up their rods for the season to hunt deer, ducks or geese. Crappie are usually densely packed and tightly related to well-defined structures. And best of all, no jet skis. Here are some tips from our experts for scoring big this winter.

DIG-THOSE DITCHES!

Ditches are the narrow grooves or indentations formed by runoff; before a reservoir was formed, they drained water from the surrounding hillsides and banks into the river and its tributaries. Ditches serve as natural migration routes that crappie use to move from deep to shallow water.

Ditch-fishin' is a favorite tactic of Kentucky Lake guide Billy Hurt. In cold water, crappie concentrate in ditches in 10 to 15 feet of water.

If the weather has been unusually mild for four or five days, the fish will move shallower along these ditches. A good place to locate these subtle structures is on a major flat. Idle around the structure, watch your depth finder and use marker buoys to pinpoint the dropoff.

"I'm convinced crappie feel a great sense of security in these little ditches," Hurt says. "The water is typically very murky now, and visibility low. Crappie moving along the ditch will swim very close to its walls, like a miner feeling his way through a dark tunnel."

The best ditches always have cover on them, usually in the form of brush, Billy has found. "Once you've located the ditch, use your trolling motor to move jigs rigged on multiple rods along it at a steady pace — not too fast, not too slow. You want to keep your lines angled back with no slack or bag. If there is any slack, waves will wash lines into your trolling motor prop and you'll have a real mess on your hands.

TUBE-AND-MINNOW TACTICS

Most crappie guides use either a soft plastic tube jig or a live minnow. Garry Mason uses both in combination to tempt sluggish slabs during the winter period.

"Kentucky Lake usually undergoes a five-foot drawdown beginning in late fall." Mason notes. "By winter, crappie have moved out of their shallow haunts into deeper water, using channels and ditches as migration routes. I'm convinced the drawdown makes them relate very tight to cover. In winter, crappie will hold very tight to a submerged stump, brushpile or tree — tighter than at any other time of year. They also have a noticeably smaller strike zone now, and if you aren't in it, you're gonna haul water.

Mason's main structures now are creek channel dropoffs that fall from 12 to about 18 feet. "The best ones invariably cut close to a submerged bar or island, and have cover associated with them at intervals along their route. This is your chance to get into big schools of megaslabs on a single clump of brush or a lone stump. For some reason, crappie really get together in a big way in cold water. Catch one fish and you're likely to catch a dozen more from the exact same spot, if you play your cards right."

Garry uses a tight-line presentation with a variation of the Kentucky rig, combining a live tuffy minnow on a tube jig's hook. "The minnow kicks and flutters and activates the tube. The tube in turn adds mass and a dash of color to your presentation, helping the crappie to locate it quickly in turbid water."

After pinpointing and marking the creek channel, use your trolling motor to traverse it slowly, working the jigs vertically. "Fish very close to cover now — the strike zone is tiny, and missing it by an inch is as good as a mile. The Kentucky rig lets you know when you're in brush. The heavy sinker telegraphs a solid tap up your line when it contacts wood; by lowering it into the brush and reeling it slowly upwards through the branches, you can find where the fish are holding without constantly hanging up. If you do get hung, break your line and rerig. I use 12 lb. mono because it's heavy enough to hold up well in brush and withstands the weight of that heavy sinker, but it's light enough so you can bust it without disturbing the crappie lair. You don't want to be popping off limbs and branches in an effort to get your rig back; this will cause the crappie school to take off like a covey of quail. Once I lower the rig into the brush, I jiggle the rod tip *sideways,* not up and down. If you use the standard up-and-down jigging stroke, your lure will be out of the strike zone much of the time."

PROBING DEEP DROPS

Steve McCadams says, "To find crappie any time of year, you've first got to find their food source. It's my theory that baitfish get nervous about being too shallow during the winter months. Winter weather in the Sun Belt can be extremely volatile — on Kentucky Lake, it's liable to be 55 degrees and sunny at noon on Monday, rain two inches Monday afternoon and get down to 20 degrees by Tuesday morning. Rapid chilling of the upper layer of water can cause massive baitfish kills — you'll go out the morning after one of these monster fronts and see dead threadfin shad carpeting the lake."

Some baitfish will always wander shallow, which usually turns into a death march when a front rolls through. "But in winter, you can always find a great number of baitfish in deep water. By staying deep, they buffer themselves against the chilling (and potentially lethal) effects of severe frontal passages. And where there's lots of bait, there's crappie."

Now is an ideal time to probe deep ledges, Steve knows. "The old creek or river channel seldom falls straight off into deep water; it drops gradually in a series of steps, a.k.a. ledges. In winter, I've found crappie will relate strongest to ledges between 18 and 25 ft. deep. I seldom catch quality fish shallower than 15 ft. now."

Stumps and brushpiles located along the ledge will attract baitfish and hold crappie. Steve fishes this scattered cover vertically with a heavy Kentucky rig (1 ounce bell sinker on the bottom) baited with live tuffies. He uses 20 pound mono for the main line, 17 to 20 for the leader. "This is a bottom- and wood-intensive saturation method, and lighter line just doesn't hold up. Besides, we're talking murky water here, so line visibility isn't a factor. I fish the rig on a

WINTER CRAPPIE PATTERNS

medium-action spinning or baitcasting outfit, much preferring the hands-on contact you get with a rod and reel over a pole in a holder. Move along the drop and tap, tap, tap that sinker around those deep ledges. Fish it slowly and carefully — this is a touchy-feely technique. When you feel the rig knock on wood, get ready for a bite.

Some days they want a jig, and when they do, Steve gives 'em a tube bait rigged on a 1/8, even a 1/4 ounce head. This heavy head/light line combo helps keep the lure straight under the boat, a blessing on rough, windy days. He fishes it vertically on 6 pound mono, and finds this setup especially good for crappie suspending off the drop in open water.

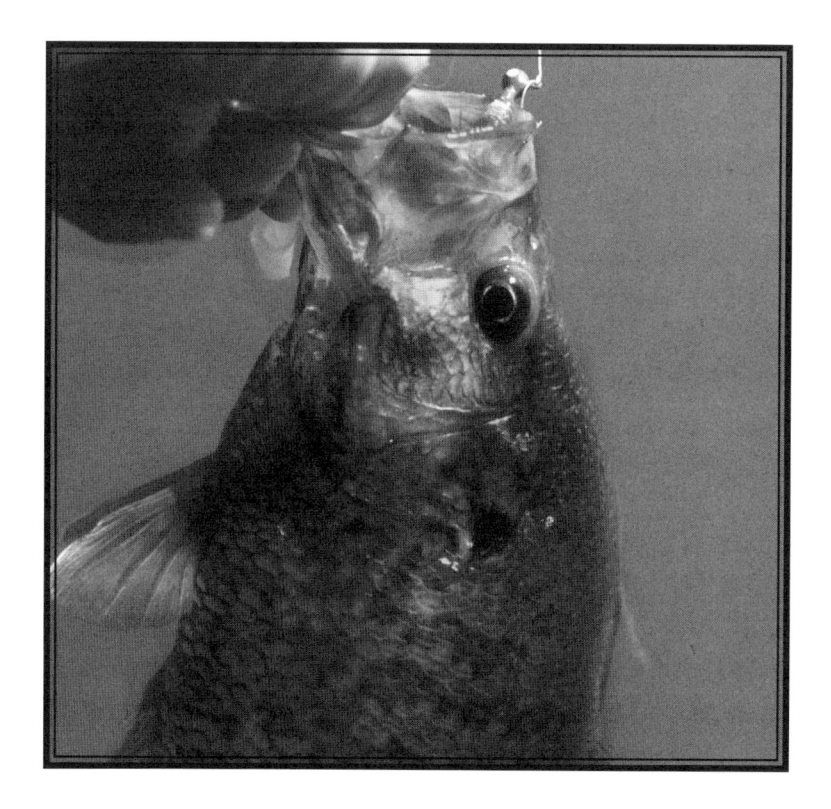

When the lake water is cold and crappie suspend, two crappie on one trolling pass is a common occurrence for guide Fred McClintock.

AGGRESSIVE TROLLING FOR COLD-WATER CRAPPIE

No, you won't find crappie fishermen on the water during late winter and early spring. Even in the Sun Belt, weather conditions can be downright brutal, with 20-degree air temperatures and howling north winds. The water is likely to be transparent one day, muddy from an overnight flood the next. And that's before the ice storm blows through! Last March, while gunning for prespawn crappie at Kentucky Lake, I had to pour lantern fuel on the launch ramp and light it to melt the ice before I could load my boat on its trailer.

Fred McClintock is exactly the kind of guy you'd expect to find searching for crappie during the tough prespawn period. He approaches fishing like safecracking: he knows there's a treasure for the taking if you can just crack the code. And he's designed the most innovative strategy for frigid-water crappie going.

Ultimate Challenge

"Unlike some of the other reservoirs in the midsouth, Dale Hollow is not known for its crappie fishing," McClintock stated. "It's deep, rocky, clear as air, and has very little wood cover." In fact, Fred never even bothered fishing for crappies until fairly recently. "I was looking for a late winter/early spring alternative for my clients, something fun to fish for on days when the smallmouth bass weren't biting. That's when I decided to check out the lake's crappie fishery."

Through considerable time on the water, much of it by himself on days so nasty that his guide trips cancelled, McClintock has fine-tuned a unique approach to prespawn crappie that involves what he calls "aggressive trolling." Unlike the brush-beating, shallow-water approaches used in spawning season, this breakthrough method involves scouring large areas of open water for suspending fish. The proof is in the pudding: Fred and his clients have boated unbelievable catches of crappie in water as cold as 36 degrees! And some of these fish have been superslabs weighing nearly 4 pounds!

"Open-water crappie are largely ignored by anglers," Fred explained. "Most crappie fans mentally associate this fish with wood cover, and can't imagine catching them more than a cast away from a brushpile or stake bed. I had never fished for crappie that much, so I wasn't hindered by these preconceived notions. These methods will work on your home lake in prespawn, but you have to keep an open mind to try them."

Seeking Suspenders

Fred usually begins chasing crappie in mid to late February. "My tipoff that it's crappie time comes when the lake has reached its coldest temperature

AGGRESSIVE TROLLING FOR COLD-WATER CRAPPIES

of the winter, normally 36 to 38 degrees, then is hit by one of the hard rains typical of this region in February and early March. Overnight the lake turns murky and its temperature rises 3 to 5 degrees. This triggers crappie that were wintering in the main body of the reservoir in deep water to pull up stakes. Normally they'll move en masse toward inflowing tributaries in the upper end of the lake, where they stack up for a brief period around whatever remnants of wood cover they can find. This pattern is quickly trashed by the inevitable blockbuster cold front that blows in behind the rainstorm. The wind shifts out of the north, air temperatures plummet and bluebird skies set in, sending the fish packing for open water…and *that's* when you can consistently catch the biggest crappie of the year."

The first major cold front following a sudden lake warmup often sends crappie into the 20 to 30 foot zone in open water, McClintock has found. He locates these fish by idling his boat in big, lazy S-shaped patterns at the mouths of tributaries, watching his graph intently for signs of crappie or baitfish schools. "Bait is a necessity now, and usually no problem to find. Most reservoirs, including Dale Hollow, are full of young-of-the-year shad and immature pelagic baitfish. I've noticed that in late winter, baitfish schools are often smack in the middle of the water column. It's you're in 30 feet of water, the bait is likely to be at 15; if you're in 50 feet, 25. And where you'll find bait, you'll find suspending crappie."

McClintock's Trolling-Setup

McClintock's 20-foot aluminum boat is custom-rigged for aggressive crappie trolling. It's equipped with 24-volt hand-steer trolling motors at both bow and stern, each with depth finder transducers attached.

An elevated trolling board contains eight rodholders; a spider rig rod holder is mounted to the front deck. Two depth finders and a surface temperature meter round out the equipment package.

When McClintock has two clients aboard, he stations them in fishing chairs on opposite sides of the rear deck and fishes six long, flexible spinning rods (12-footers mounted in holders at the front, 10-footers out the back). He spools his reels with Berkley SensiThin mono, which he prefers for its resistance to coiling in cold water, in varying tests from 8 to 12 pounds. "Besides slab crappie, we catch smallmouths, spotted bass, walleyes, catfish, even an occasional musky with this method, and seldom get broken off with these whippy rods," Fred noted. "There's never any doubt when you've got a fish — the rod bends halfway over." Each stick is rigged with two lures: either a diving crankbait and a tube or twister jig positioned above the crank on a 3-way swivel, or two jigs.

Initial Warmup Pattern

After determining the depth of the crappie/baitfish school, McClintock lets out from 1 to 2 cast-lengths of line behind his boat and begins power trolling through the area at speeds up to 2 1/2 mph. He crisscrosses the width of the tributary in a lazy S pattern, finding the majority of his fish relating to baitfish, not bottom structure — "More like a hybrid or striper pattern than a crappie pattern," as he puts it. "The object is to present multiple lures from 5 to 15 feet deep and quickly determine the right presentation that'll trigger the school into action." Depth of the presentations can be controlled by the size/style of crankbait, jig weight and line diameter used. "For my deepest presentations, I use quarter-ounce deep-diving crankbaits like Mann's 15+; other depth zones are covered by using 1/8-ounce medium and shallow divers."

Crappie are incredibly color-selective in cold, clear water; once McClintock starts picking up fish, he immediately replaces lure colors that aren't working with those that are. If the bite slacks off, he'll reel in and try new colors, constantly experimenting with different combinations throughout the day.

Early in the season, bigger fish normally hit the crankbaits, while more fish bite the jigs, Fred said. "The crankbait bite is my favorite; this is fast, fun fishing. Some days the big boys will really whack it. But as the water warms, the crank bite gradually tapers off. Then I'll use crankbaits strictly as depth planers to get my jigs down."

Fine-Tuning the Approach

The mood of the fish and ever-changing lake conditions dictate McClintock's trolling approach. "As the season progresses and the water temp rises, crappie move upward in the water column, further back into the tributary arms and closer to shore. It doesn't take much of a warmup to make 'em move, either. One day last spring, the lake temp was 40 degrees in the morning and we were catching crappie 15 feet deep. By noon the water had warmed to 42 degrees and the fish had moved up to 7 feet. But on days when the wind shifts out of the north or east, the reverse may occur."

The guide occasionally runs into a school of crappie that refuse to bite a trolled lure. He then reverts to a tactic he calls "stalling." "After rigging all your rods with jigs, circle back around the school, put your trolling motor on high-24 until you're smokin' along, then kill the motor. This causes the jigs to sink s-l-o-w-l-y through the school. We've had 10 fish on at once with this method." In the unlikely event stalling fails, Fred stops his boat near the school and casts a 1/16-ounce jig to the suspending fish. "Usually it won't make it to the bottom without a crappie nailing it."

Once the jig bite becomes prevalent, usually in water around 48 degrees, Fred fine-tunes his presentation even further. "I often run 1/8 ounce jigs on the bottom and 1/16 ounce above — I like to use the heaviest lures I can get away with when power trolling, and this is a killer combination up to 2 mph. But when the fish aren't aggressive, I'll fish lighter jigs (perhaps 1/16 on bottom and 1/32 on top) and slow down to 1 mph. I keep dropping back in lure size and boat speed until the fish react positively."

McClintock seldom lets a spring cold front ruin a crappie trip. "If you're faced with a bluebird sky and a sudden temperature drop, look for murky water, reduce your bait size and slow your troll. Stalling works great during cold fronts. Often the lake rises quickly after a spring deluge — this is when our smallmouth fishermen catch giant crappie on bass lures. Try trolling parallel to deep banks."

Aggressive trolling is not the laid-back approach most crappie anglers are used to. "It's a non-stop fire drill," McClintock laughed. "I'm constantly rigging lures, switching jig weight combinations and changing colors, but we spend plenty of time reeling in fish, too."

MORE PRESPAWN TROLLING SAVVY

- Try to present your lures just above the level of the fish. If you're graphing crappies but aren't scoring strikes, your lures are probably running below the school.

Speed up your troll, run lighter lures, use heavier line or let less line out to reach shallow fish.

- A graph rigged with two transducers, one pointed down and one to the side, is a big help in locating wandering crappie schools in open water.

- Crappie are highly color selective. On sunny days when the water is clear, baitfish-imitating hues such as white, silver and gray often draw the most strikes; try fire tiger, chartreuse, brown, orange and red on overcast days and in murky water.

- Crappie often stack up at mudlines formed when runoff enters a tributary following a hard rain. Run up a clear creek arm until you find murky water, then troll this edge.

- If you're only catching small fish, increase your lure size. Tiny tube baits will catch plenty of keepers, but crankbaits will score the biggest fish.

Jigs are simple, yet deadly lures that can catch crappie in endless ways.

ADVANCED JIGGING TACTICS

The leadhead jig is unquestionably the deadliest artificial lure ever created for crappie. Extreme versatility is the key to its success. You can fish jigs 12 months of the year in an astounding number of crappie situations by varying their style, weight, color and presentation. And, you can pack a zillion jigs in your tackle bag and still have plenty of room for a baloney sandwich!

Serious crappie anglers are always looking for new wrinkles in jig fishing. Here, some of the top crappie guides in the nation share their secret jigging methods – tactics you can use to score more and bigger crappie on your next outing.

TOM MOODY'S COLD FRONT APPROACH

Tom Moody, like other veteran Kentucky Lake crappie guides, uses the Kentucky rig for probing this sprawling reservoir's ledges, dropoffs and submerged brushpiles. Tom uses a standard double wire crappie rig with a 3/4-ounce bell sinker on the bottom. Moody normally prepares the rig with two hooks baited with shiner minnows, but during cold fronts, he replaces one or both hooks with a Charlie Brewer Slider Grub on a 1/16-ounce jighead.

You'd think live bait would outperform any artificial lure during a severe cold front, but you'd be wrong, Moody insists. "The Slider Grub can be fished just as slowly and methodically as live shiners, but it gives you the added versatility of using color to your advantage," he indicated. "By mixing and matching grub and jighead colors, you can achieve exactly the right presentation to trigger bites from non-aggressive fish."

Crappie are more color-sensitive than most other freshwater gamefish, including bass, Moody emphasized. "Often merely changing jig colors provokes an immediate aggressive feeding response. That's why pays to keep plenty of Slider Grub, tube bait or twister grub color options in your tacklebox, and to experiment with different jighead/lure color combinations. These lures are inexpensive; you can equip a couple of plastic utility boxes with a complete color palette for under twenty bucks. Be sure to stock up on different colored jigheads while you're at it — sometimes just changing from a white to a chartreuse head will turn the fish on."

Cold-front crappie often bury deep inside brushpiles and stake beds; this presents no problem for Moody's modified Kentucky rig. "Simply position the boat directly over the cover, lower the sinker to the bottom, reel your line up slowly, then lower it back into the cover," he instructed. "Determine whether the crappie are striking the top or bottom hook/jig, then adjust your presentation accordingly. For example, if most of your hits are coming on the jig, replace the live bait hook with another Slider Grub in the same or a different color. When fishing two jigs, if your hits are coming mostly on the top lure, raise the level of your presentation a foot or so; often this results in two crappie striking the rig at once."

Tom's Bonus Tip: "When rigging a soft plastic bait on a jighead, always position the knot on the hook eye so the lure hangs at a 90-degree angle from the rod tip. This gives the jig the natural look of a live minnow swimming horizontally through the water."

GARRY MASON'S SUSPENDING CRAPPIE TECHNIQUE

There's no question that a jig's single hook and compact lead head make it a good choice for probing dense bottom cover. But this lure is also an effective tool for catching crappie suspending in the water column – especially once you master Garry Mason's unusual presentation tactic, that is.

"The problem most anglers have with jigging suspending crappie is keeping the jig within the depth zone the fish are using," Mason pointed out. "Many fishermen have experienced the frustration of catching a fat crappie from a suspending school, only to be unable to score repeat strikes because they couldn't put their jig back in front of the fish."

Mason's technique revolves around the spinning reels he uses on his crappie rods. "Say I just hooked a crappie 18 feet deep off the side of a creek channel," he explained. "I know I want to get my jig back in that same spot as quickly as possible, and the surest way to do that is to not touch the reel handle while bringing in the fish. So instead of reeling, the instant I feel the fish hit, I squeeze the line closest to my right hand tightly against the rod handle, then reach down and pull the line above the handle far enough so I can get the fish up to within reach of the landing net. I then unhook the fish and drop my jig back into the exact same depth zone. This will seem awkward at first, but with practice, it becomes easy, and it's the surest way to jig up a boatload of suspending crappie I know of."

Garry's bonus tip: "When fishing a jig vertically, it's critical to have your line as vertical as possible, not at an extreme angle from the boat. If the wind is blowing hard enough to offset your line angle, go to a heavier jighead, or pinch one or two split shot about 3 inches above your lure."

JIM DUCKWORTH'S TROLLING METHOD

This tip is ideal for you crappie anglers who get easily bored when sitting on a hole and waiting for the fish to bite. "I've had excellent results over the years trolling crankbaits for white bass, walleye and sauger, and discovered along the way that crappie would often respond to a trolling presentation as well, especially from post-spawn through summer," Jim noted. "In order to make my trolling presentation more crappie-specific, I came up with a rig that incorporates both a crankbait and a jig."

Duckworth ties on a Bandit 200 crankbait, the adds a 1/16-ounce Slider Grub to the trailing hook via a leader line. "This rig is awesome when crappie are suspending in open water over a channel dropoff or hump, or relating loosely to deep submerged brushpiles," he explained. "The crankbait works like a depth planer to get the jig down to the level of the fish, and then keeps it at a constant level.

I'll locate a school of crappie or a big wad of bait on my graph, then circle back around and slow-troll through it with my gas outboard or trolling motor."

On days when crappie are actively feeding, it's not unusual to hang fish on both lures at the same time, Jim said. "But the jig part of the rig really shines when the bite is slow," he added. "The Slider Grub is a compact, non-threatening offering that even sluggish crappie can't turn down."

Jim's bonus tip: "Even when crappie won't hit the crankbait, it serves as an attractor, getting their attention until the jig swims by. For maximum visibility, change crankbait colors to match water conditions. In murky water, use a bright color such as chartreuse, hot orange or hot orange. But in clear water, go for realism and flash with a shad or chrome pattern. Replace the stock front treble hook on your crankbait with a red hook for even more attraction."

HAROLD MORGAN'S FLOAT 'N FLY METHOD

The so-called float 'n fly is a combination of a plastic bobber and a small hair jig that has taken winter smallmouth bass fishermen by storm. This innocent-looking rig is incredibly deadly on bass suspending in cold, clear water, and although the jigs used with the method are miniscule, it's racked up impressive catches of trophy smallmouths in many cold-weather bass tournaments.

Although the float 'n fly has received plenty of national press as a hot new bass technique, it's really a time-tested crappie method, one Harold Morgan has used for decades. "This is the ultimate jigging method for suspending crappie," Harold promised. "Virtually all other jig presentations involve some movement of the lure, either sideways or up and down in the water column. Not this one. The bobber floats the jig in place indefinitely, which is exactly the presentation you want when the water is gin-clear and super-cold."

Morgan turns to the float 'n fly when the water temperature dips below 50 degrees in winter, noting, "It really comes into its own in 40- to 45-degree water, when crappie typically refuse to bite even live bait."

Harold uses a long, light-action spinning outfit spooled with 6 pound mono, 4 if the water is extra-clear. He ties a 1/16-ounce hair jig to the end of his line, trims the hair back with scissors so it's about even with the bend of the hook, snaps a small plastic bobber on the line and positions it from 8 to 12 feet above the jig.

Morgan fishes the float rig on banks with a rapid slope into deep water, such as a channel bluff. He casts the bobber close to the structure, waits several seconds for the jig to sink, then either lets the bobber sit still, or gently shakes his rod tip to make the bobber (and the jig) quiver in place. If nothing happens after a minute or so, he reels in a couple of feet of line and dangles the jig some more. It usually doesn't take long for the crappie to react. "The tiny jig looks just like a fry minnow, and crappie will attack it without hesitation. It'll also catch bass, trout and walleye. This rig proves that in jig fishing, sometimes less action is more desirable."

CHOOSING JIGHEAD WEIGHT

Jigheads come in a wide variety of weights. Which weight you should be using depends on a number of factors, including depth of the structure you're fishing, depth of the crappie or baitfish displayed on your graph, activity of the fish (i.e. is the bite slow or fast?), wind velocity, and what line test/rod action you're using.

"If the only object were to get the jig to the bottom as fast a possible, you'd want to use a heavy jig, say 1/2 ounce," Duckworth pointed out. "But there's a lot more to jiggin' crappie than getting your lure to the bottom. A jig's rate of fall is vital to how the fish react to it. In most crappie situations, a 1/16 or 1/8 ounce jighead will have the slow to moderate fall rate that'll make your presentation appear totally lifelike to the fish. Beyond that, take into account depth of the fish and wind velocity. If the crappie are 10 feet deep and there's no wind, a 1/16 ounce head will work fine, but that's not enough weight if the wind's blowing 15 mph and the crappie are 20 feet deep – then you'd want to switch to a 1/8 or 3/16-ounce head. If the fish are even deeper and the wind is stronger, try a quarter-ounce head."

As a rule of thumb, the less active the crappie, the lightest jighead you should use – within reason, of course. "Lethargic fish will strike something falling very slowly past their noses, but won't go out of their way to chase down something that shoots rapidly past them," Jim said. "On the other hand, you can't cast a 1/100-ounce jig on a crappie rod. I'd suggest stocking up with 1/16, 1/8, 3/16 and 1/4-ounce heads; these should cover 99% of the crappie scenarios you're likely to encounter."

As reservoirs age, wood cover disappears, and sinking your own cover becomes critical to crappie angling success.

HAROLD MORGAN'S SECRETS FOR SINKING COVER

In my many outings with Harold Morgan, I've been constantly amazed at his ability to catch crappie when other anglers on the lake are shooting blanks. This veteran guide has refined his live bait and lure techniques over decades of crappie fishing, yet insists that without painstaking preparation well before the crappie season begins, even the most sophisticated rigs and presentations cannot produce to their full potential. For Harold, this preparation means sinking crappie cover in his home lakes.

"Most fishermen think dropping a Christmas tree or two in the lake is all it takes to ensure good crappie fishing, but there's much more to it than that," Morgan insists. Here, the guide reveals his secrets for sinking cover — secrets you can use to greatly enhance crappie waters near you!

But first, a word of caution: sinking brush, trees or other types of cover is not legal everywhere. Check state and local regulations first.

Why Sink Cover?

Morgan says if you're serious about catching crappie year-'round, it's important to sink cover. He lists several reasons why:

- *Aging reservoirs* — "As our reservoirs get older, their submerged wood cover disappears," Morgan explained. "Trees and brush rot away, get broken up by wave action and scattered by anglers who hang lures and anchors in it, or wash away in current. No new reservoirs have been constructed in years, so the cover in our aging reservoirs needs replacing."

- *Baitfish magnet* — "Wood cover draws baitfish. They feed on the algae which coats the wood, and find shelter from predators in the shadows of the cover. More baitfish means more crappie."

- *Current break* — "In rivers and river-run reservoirs, wood cover provides a current break which can draw in scores of crappie."

- *Spawning aid* — "Crappie spawn around submerged wood. I've seen females press against the forks of branches to help them lay their eggs."

- *Secret spots* — "By sinking cover and carefully noting its location, you can have your own secret honey holes and catch fish even when other anglers are hauling water."

Which Wood Works

In their attempts at luring crappie, some anglers plant stake beds; others sink brushpiles; still others drop Christmas trees. Morgan uses dead trees or large branches for crappie cover; he prefers sections of hardwood, willow and fruit trees: "These varieties last a long time in the water — I'm still fishing some trees today that I sank over 12 years ago!"

Christmas trees and cedar trees? No way, Morgan insists. "The single biggest mistake I see crappie anglers who are sinking cover make is relying too much on pines and cedars. I believe these trees put out an aroma which can repel fish. Their bushy branches get mired down with silt so the tree gets pressed down flat; this explains why you often can't locate the Christmas tree you sank last winter once spring rolls around. And their branches are so full, fish cannot move freely within the tree, and you stay hung up constantly when fishing them."

Never put out any tree or large branch with its leaves still attached, the guide warns. "The leaves stay there for a surprisingly long time, and grab silt like a catcher's mitt."

Morgan's Method

Morgan searches for wood on the banks of Priest and Old Hickory when these reservoirs are at their lowest level, usually from December through late February. "Two winters ago we had a massive ice storm, and we're still picking up dead branches and entire trees that were downed. There's usually plenty of dead wood on the ground, so never cut down live trees."

Although it is often necessary to trim a large branch to make it more manageable when dragging it to the water's edge, Morgan always leaves at least a couple of primary limbs attached. "These elevate the trunk off the bottom, so crappie and baitfish have plenty of room to roam about freely underneath. A tree whose trunk is elevated will produce far more fish than one laying flat on the bottom."

Harold uses a bow saw to cut downed wood into a manageable size; they prefer trees and branches from 18 to 22 feet in length. "This is small enough to be easily handled by one or two persons, yet long enough so that when you sink it, you can position your boat parallel to the tree and everyone in the boat can fish the cover," Harold points out. "If you sank a 10-foot tree, the angler in the back of the boat may not be able to reach it."

Once a likely tree or branch is located, Morgan enlists a fishing partner to help him drag it to the water's edge. Next, he cuts two 6-foot sections of stout nylon rope and attach one near the middle and the other at the thickest end. "These lines are used to connect your weight to the tree," Morgan explains. "Nylon rope lasts a long time and holds a knot well. The tag end of each rope section is tied into a loop or 'pigtail'; this makes it easier to attach the weight quickly."

A longer piece of rope is next tied near the end of the trunk; this is attached to a boat cleat. After double-checking all connections, Morgan slowly backs his boat away from shore and drags the tree into the water. Then his partner pulls the tree closer to the boat and uses the short pigtail ropes to snug the branches close to the side. A plastic tarp or old blanket is used to prevent the limbs from scratching the fiberglass.

With the tree secured alongside the boat, Morgan idles to the spot where he wants to drop the tree; this location has been previously marked with a marker buoy. While Harold keeps the boat steady (no easy feat on a windy day), his buddy attaches a heavy concrete block to one of the pigtail ropes, then drops that end of the tree into the water. He repeats this process with the other end, and the cover sinks to the bottom.

WHERE TO SINK TREES

Morgan says knowing the best places to sink cover can ensure great crappie fishing 12 months out of the year. "The first factor you must take into account is the difference between low and full pool at your local reservoir. Priest Lake, for example, is 5 to 7 feet higher at full pool than during its lowest drawdown point in winter. If I want my tree to be in 15 feet of water in spring once the lake level rises, then I'll have to sink it in 8 to 10 feet of water in the winter."

Shallow trees are easy targets for other anglers, Morgan has found. "If I want to fish a tree in 8 feet of water in spring, this means I have to sink it in only 1 to 3 feet of water in winter; some of the branches will stick above the surface before the lake fills up, making it easy for my competition to spot." Although most anglers may prefer to fish shallower cover, Morgan has found trees in the 15- to 17-foot range will produce crappie nearly year-'round, while remaining hidden from other anglers.

The guide carefully plans where and how deep he sinks his trees. "I vary my 'drop spots' so I have good year-'round coverage," he says. "I presently have over 300 trees out in Priest Lake alone; some produce in spring, others in fall, still others in summer and winter." Here are some places Morgan recommends as prime spots for sinking cover:

- *Deep points* — "These are terrific summer spots; suspending crappie will move onto points when feeding. Avoid sinking the tree on the very tip of the point, for this is a frequent casting target of bass fishermen, who will hang their worms and crankbaits in the branches and quickly break up the cover. Instead, sink it on the deepest side from 15 to 20 feet deep."

- *Creek channel dropoffs* — "Crappie use narrow creek channels like highways when moving around the reservoir. Sink some trees on the high side of the dropoff 10-15 feet deep, and others with the trunk in the channel itself and the branches angling up to the top of the ledge. Use two cement blocks on the deep end of the cover or it may wash away during floods. Always sink a few trees all the way down into the channel; these will produce in the dead of winter."

- *Flats* — "Flats with sand and pebbles on the bottom are good spawning sites, and a well-placed tree in this area will draw a ton of fat spawners. Drop a few trees from 10 to 20 feet deep near the very edge of the flat, close to a channel dropoff."

- *Humps* — "These will pull crappie in during the summer and fall. Bass fishermen usually hammer the top of the hump with their lures, so keep your trees on the deeper sides and ends. This is a good place to angle a tree from deep to shallow water for maximum depth coverage."

- *Boat docks* — "A single tree sunk in 15 to 20 feet of water near your boat dock can produce plenty of crappie spring through fall."

Preparation Pays

Sinking cover is hard work. But as Harold Morgan puts it, "It's like taking out a crappie insurance policy. A few trees in the right places will help guarantee success for years to come."

MAKE YOUR COVER COUNT

Harold takes sinking cover seriously. Here's how he makes sure all his hard work pays off.

- *Keep a low profile--* Be secretive about where you drop your trees. Don't sink a tree when other anglers are watching.

- *Chart your trees* — Mark a map showing the location of every tree you drop — don't rely on your memory. A GPS unit is a tremendous asset when fishing sunken cover; record GPS coordinates in a logbook after you sink the tree.

- *Isolate some trees* — Sometimes a single tree dropped on a rather featureless piece of cover will produce more fish than a large tangle of trees. Isolated trees pull in crappie from a wide area.

- *Vary rope lengths* —When sinking multiple trees, vary the length of the ropes to which your cement blocks are attached. While 6 feet is a good average, make some lines shorter and some longer. The trees will often float up from the blocks.

- *Sink plenty of trees* — Having lots of trees to choose from keeps you from overfishing any one tree and assures you plenty of choices should other anglers locate some of your cover.

- *Safety first* — Don't try to move a big tree with a small boat, and never overload the boat with cement blocks. Always wear your PFD when sinking trees.

Crappie are where you find them. Jim Duckworth caught these fish from a tiny state park lake.

CATCH CRAPPIE IN UNEXPECTED PLACES

Many of our nation's reservoirs and natural lakes hold tremendous populations of crappie, so it's little wonder most of the fishing pressure directed at our favorite fish takes place on these large bodies of water. But crappie are highly adaptable critters, and it may some as a surprise to learn that you can catch them from places you've probably never considered fishing. I asked the experts about these unexpected crappie haunts. What you're about to learn will open your eyes to unexploited crappie fishing possibilities close to home where you just might tangle with a wall-hanger fish.

Up The Creek

Garry Mason plies his guiding trade a 160,000-acre Kentucky Lake. But when he's not guiding clients on "The Big Pond," he's exploring the many creeks and streams near his home for...guess what?

"Most anglers are shocked to learn that you can find great crappie action in creeks," Mason indicated. "But remember, the steams were there before the dam was built and a reservoir was formed, and crappie were swimming in them back then as they are now. I grew up fishing creeks, and there's nothing I enjoy more today than creek fishin' with my boys. Many anglers today have gotten away from this simple way of fishing, but there's no better way to get away from the pressures of everyday life — and catch some quality crappie while you're at it."

Mason discovered years ago that many crappie will run up creeks feeding into Kentucky Lake and other reservoirs during the spawning season. "This annual migration occurs most commonly when the water is high due to seasonal rains and the raising of the lake level to summer pool," he said. "There's more water in the tributaries then, enabling crappie to run a country mile up a feeder creek until they reach an area that's suitable for spawning. Of course, not all the crappie in the lake will run up the creeks – many will remain in the bays, coves and brushy tributary arms to spawn. But if exploring new crappie territory rings your chimes like it does mine, there's no better place to start than a shallow inflowing creek."

Both water temperature and dissolved oxygen levels play key roles in this migration, Mason said. "Crappie instinctively seek out the best habitat for spawning, and in spring, creeks flowing into a reservoir often run considerably warmer than the main lake, and are usually higher in dissolved oxygen. Thus crappie will often spawn earlier in a creek than they will in the main lake. Start fishing creeks in early spring, and keep moving up them as the season progresses."

Some streams and creeks can be fished from a small boat; others, you'll have to wade, Mason pointed out. "I'll often run my boat as far up a tributary arm as possible, then beach it and wade the stream from there. Crappie are crappie, whether they're in a creek or a massive reservoir; they like wood cover and clear to stained, as opposed to muddy, water. Fortunately you'll always find plenty of wood to fish in a creek: logjams, flooded bushes, stickups and mats of floating debris that gather in eddies will all hold crappie. And even when creeks get muddy after a hard rain, they usually clear up quickly."

Mason finds good crappie fishing near the juncture of two creek arms, in slack water at the ends of gravel bars and in deep holes where the current is slowed. Concerning the latter, he emphasized that "deep" is a relative term: "The deepest water in the creek you're fishing may be only 3 or 4 feet, if that. The rule of thumb I use is, if it's over the top of my waders, it's plenty deep for crappie!"

Mason's favorite rig for creek crappie is a small tube jig or live minnow suspended beneath a float. "Adjust the float so the jig or minnow is just off bottom, cast the rig slightly upstream of a brushpile or logjam, then let it float down to your target. Often creek water is super-clear and the fish are tight to cover and extremely spooky; I like to let the bobber float right against the cover. Also, avoid putting too much action on the float and lure with the rod tip; a simple dead-stick approach often pays off better in this situation."

Creek fishermen may be treated to a most amazing sight: crappie feeding on the surface, Garry added. "It's more like a trout surfacing than a bass; just a subtle rise with hardly any splash, but it's really neat to witness. Of course, this should come as great news to the fly-rodder – you can wrack up a nice mess of creek crappie with a sponge spider or a small popping bug."

Secondary Lakes

With most crappie-fishing attention focused on large bodies of water, it's no wonder that smaller angling venues often remain underfished – and full of slab crappie. Such is often the case with state park lakes, county and municipal lakes, "borrow" pits formed during highway construction, and other so-called "secondary" lakes. Harold Morgan makes a practice of sniffing out these overlooked hotspots, and has found they can offer good to excellent crappie fishing, as well as a chance to escape the crowds. "These days it seems everybody has a boat with a big outboard on the transom, and they want to fish places where they can put the hammer down and speed from one hole to the next," Morgan pointed out. "Many secondary lakes have outboard restrictions; others lack launch ramps and must be fished from shore, or waded. If you've invested a big wad of money in a boat, chances are you're not going to bother fishing these places. But they have a reputation for producing monster crappie. The 4 pound, 4 ounce Tennessee state record black crappie came from an obscure state-managed lake you can practically jump across."

Many small public lakes are stocked with crappie; the best producers in terms of both numbers and size tend to cover at least 10 acres and have some deep water – the deeper, the better, Harold said. "For crappie, I like a small lake with some 18 to 30 foot water; this helps enable the fish to survive harsh winters and provides a more suitable habitat for threadfin shad, the crappie's preferred forage. Not all secondary public lakes I've fished meet these criteria, but the ones that do tend to be super crappie fisheries."

Jim Duckworth seconds Morgan's high opinion of secondary lakes. "Where permitted, a boat with a good depth finder is a huge help when exploring these mini-fisheries," he noted. "A 20- to 50-acre state park or state-managed daily-fee lake usually has the same types of structures you'd find in a huge reservoir, including flats, points, a deep channel, submerged humps, etc. My best tip for fishing these lakes is to look for what I call 'subtle structure', that is, places that aren't readily visible to the naked eye. A prime example might be a ledge running from a point back into a cove or short tributary arm, one that drops from 8 to 12 feet. I can guarantee that most angler who frequent these lakes will ignore such a spot, and will focus instead on the more obvious structures such points and flats."

Trolling a small crankbait with your electric motor is an excellent way to ascertain the lay of the land (or water) on these small fisheries, Duckworth said. "This method will allow you to cover lots of water efficiently and is capable of catching crappie that are either hugging bottom or suspended in the water column. Use your electric motor to pull a small crankbait across main-lake and tributary flats, as well as around suspended baitfish schools that may be hanging around channels and ledges. For covering depths of 10 feet or less, I recommend trolling a 200-series Bandit on 8 pound mono. I go to the larger 300-series Bandit when probing deeper water; it'll run down to 18 feet." Trolling is especially productive in post-spawn, the guide noted: "Crappie often suspend off the edges of flats then, and are suckers for a trolled crankbait."

Strip Mine Lakes

In areas of the country where coal is extensively mined, lakes formed from reclaimed strip mine pits offer tremendous sport fishing opportunities. Once mining activity is finished, many of these pits are filled with water and stocked with gamefish such as bass, catfish, and in some cases, crappie. One might raise valid concerns about the ecological implications of such mining practices, but there's no doubt about the awesome fishing that can result.

Kentucky Lake guide Steve McCadams says strip pits can produce some giant crappie. "These are often extremely clear and lack extensive wood cover; black crappie tend to do extremely well in them – this species acclimates better to clear water than white crappie. Strip mine lakes are my first choice for a non-traditional crappie venue."

Most strip mine lakes fall into two categories, Steve explained. "The first type is deep, extremely clear and often devoid of cover except for the occasional tree or brushpile that anglers have sunk. It's found in areas where the coal vein ran fairly deep. The banks of these pits are often straight up and down. Most of the crappie in them are either hanging tight to this sparse wood cover; in small, shallow cuts off the main bowl of the lake; or suspended in open water. The second type is most common where the coal vein was located close to the surface. It features a series of parallel humps, somewhat like corn rows, with their tops either sticking out of the water or covered by a foot or two of water, and a trench 10 to 12 feet deep running between the humps. These pits often become overgrown with weeds in summer, but can produce some big crappie the rest of the year."

OTHER PLACES TO CHECK OUT

Subdivision lakes – Usually better for bream and bass, but can support crappie if large and deep enough. Fish them from the bank with twister grubs or live bait under a float.

Golf course lakes – Ditto the above.

Irrigation ditches – I've heard of huge crappie being caught from irrigation ditches in eastern Arkansas. Many such ditches are deep enough to support crappie. Worth fishing in early spring; try a small spinnerbait. And watch out for snakes.

SHOULD YOU STOCK CRAPPIE IN YOUR POND?

Thousands of Americans fish farm ponds and small public ponds for bass, bluegill and catfish. But what about crappie? Are ponds a suitable habitat for this species?

Jim Duckworth has a one-acre pond in his back yard, and has had negative results with crappie. "I had some bass and bream in the pond, then a couple years ago I put in a few big crappie that I'd caught in a reservoir," Duckworh said. "Now the pond is chock full of small crappie, and all the fry that the bass and bream produce become instant crappie chow. Looks like I'm going to have to drain and restock it. Judging from my experience, I'd recommend that landowners use extreme caution before stocking crappie."

"We get a lot of questions from landowners about whether or not they should stock crappie in their ponds," said Mike Bramlett, fisheries biologist for the Tennessee Wildlife Resources Agency. "Crappie can thrive in a properly-managed pond as small as 5 acres, but we generally discourage the practice of stocking them in such waters because their population typically becomes overcrowded and stunted – instead of a reasonable population of quality fish, a massive number of 4 to 6 inch fish becomes the norm in most ponds. Plus, the majority of ponds are too shallow for crappie to survive a harsh winter."

Crappie will consume whatever minnows happen to be available in a pond, and this include copious quantities of gamefish fry, Bramlett explained. "Crappie usually spawn earlier than either bass or bluegill, and crappie fry will have grown large enough to feed on bass and bream fry once the latter two hatch. This isn't a problem on a big body of water where large populations of shad and minnows exist, but in a pond, there's usually not a large and varied food supply, and crappie will turn to gamefish fry for a meal."

BUSTING CRAPPIE FISHING'S BIGGEST MYTHS
by DON WIRTH

Hang around any marina coffee shop long enough, and you're bound to hear wildly inaccurate statements uttered about the crappie, misconceptions that even highly skilled anglers swear to be the gospel truth. Some of these myths have been ingrained in the lore of crappie fishing for so long, generations of fishermen have accepted them without question…until now, that is. Since the surest route to more successful crappie outings is to fish intelligently, so we asked our panel of experts to bust the biggest myths associated with our sport. If you've one of the thousands of crappie anglers who believe the following myths to be true, prepare to receive a dose of reality!

"Crappie Are Always Around Cover"

"If a psychologist gave a group of fishermen a word association test and said the phrase 'brushpile', 99% of them would instantly respond 'crappie'," Steve McCadams laughed. "That's how strongly this species is linked with submerged wood cover in the minds of most fishermen."

As with most myths, this one is based partly in fact. "Crappie do indeed gravitate to brushy cover much of the year," McCadams said. "When you're hauling one fish after another out of brushpiles or stake beds in April, it's easy to assume that these fish favor thick cover all year long. But, surprise — there are times when crappie don't relate to cover of any kind."

McCadams listed the prespawn and postspawn periods as times when crappie commonly shun cover. "Most anglers have trouble getting on fish during these transitional periods because the crappie aren't in what they view as classic crappie locations: shallow, brushy coves and tributaries. Instead, they're suspending in open water, a nightmare scenario for many fishermen. Prespawn crappie may stage in large numbers a country mile from the nearest brushpile, waiting for conditions to get just right before moving shallow to spawn. I've often found them hanging 15 feet deep in 25 feet of water at this time. Later, postspawn crappie backtrack to these same staging areas and hang out in open water for a spell, resting up from the rigors of procreation before heading for their summer haunts."

Catching open-water crappie requires an open mind. "Now is the time to abandon the target-fishing mentality and fish in broad strokes," McCadams suggested. "Trolling crankbaits on planer boards is a deadly tactic for suspenders, as is electric-trolling tube jigs on spider rigs across points and humps."

"Live Bait Catches More Crappie Than Lures"

"Some crappie anglers are so insistent on using live bait that they'll cancel their fishing trip if the bait shop has sold out of minnows," Garry Mason pointed out. "The more I fish for crappie, the more I'm sold on artificial lures, not only for numbers of fish, but for big fish as well."

Mason uses artificials in all seasons. His favorite lure is a 2-inch Charlie Brewer Slider Grub rigged on a 1/16th ounce jighead. "The Slider grub has a paddle tail that throbs when retrieved, sending out vibrations and strong visual cues to crappie," he said. "Paddletail grubs have more realistic action than either tube baits or twisters. My favorite colors are smoke flake, chartreuse, melon green, white and hot pink, but other hues may work better in your local waters. Unlike live minnows, soft plastic baits are cheap, so keeping a big selection on hand won't bankrupt you."

Mason usually casts and retrieves his leadhead lures as opposed to fishing them vertically. "Rather than sit in one spot waiting for the fish to bite, I use my trolling motor to move slowly along large structures such as channel ledges, flats and points while I cast lures to submerged stumps, brushpiles, stake beds and trees. It's exactly the same approach used by tournament bass fishermen, and it produces whopper crappie."

In the rare instances where grubs don't produce, Mason casts 1/8-ounce spinnerbaits and crankbaits, bumping them around stumps and stake beds.

The guide favors a slow, steady retrieve with most artificials. "Live bait fishermen who experiment with lure casting often overwork the lure with too many jerks and pumps of the rod," he indicated. "The so-called 'swimming retrieve' is by far the easiest and most effective way to consistently catch crappie on a grub. It lets the subtle, built-in action of the lure do all the work for you. Simply cast the grub past the target, let it sink to the bottom, lift the rod tip sharply to the 10 o'clock position, then reel slowly and steadily while holding the rod held perfectly still. This causes the lure to swim just like a live minnow. If you feel the lure touch cover or drag bottom, reel slightly faster. When you detect either a sharp tap or a heavy, soggy sensation, set the hook and reel in a big crappie."

Mason uses a 7-foot Lamiglas #702 ultralight spinning rod, a stick he claims will routinely cast a 1/16-ounce grub 40 feet. "Don't sell that whippy rod short when it comes to fish-fighting power!" he stressed. "I've landed 7-pound largemouth bass and 10-pound catfish on it."

"You Can't Put Pressure on a Hooked Crappie"

"Somewhere along the line the crappie picked up the unfortunate nickname 'papermouth', and this has led to the cancellation of countless fish dinners," Steve McCadams said. "Many anglers play a crappie like they're walking on eggshells, and this leads to too many fish coming unhooked — or never being hooked in the first place."

While it's true that they shouldn't be jerked out of the water and banged against the side of the boat the way those tv bass pros do with their fish, crappie, especially fat females, needn't be babied. "Many fishermen are so careful about tearing that so-called paper mouth that they're afraid to set the hook when they get a bite," McCadams noted. "Counting on the fish to hook itself is usually a losing proposition. Fishing for crappie is one thing; catching them requires a firm hookset."

The instant a bite is detected, McCadams suggests flicking the wrist holding the rod. "Don't haul off and hammer the fish — just a simple wrist-flick will move the rod tip sufficiently to bury the hook barb, provided your hook has a sharp point. Then, keep the rod tip high while reeling at a moderate speed; this will move the fish away from cover into open water without ripping out the hook. Many crappie flop on the surface when trying to escape; this is when a fish that hasn't been hooked solidly is most likely to come unbuttoned. The unfortunate angler is then left to believe that the hook ripped through the crappie's mouth, when in fact the hook probably never penetrated the mouth in the first place."

The right rod is mandatory for a good hookset. McCadams' favorite crappie stick is a 6 1/2 foot medium-action G. Loomis spinning rod. "It has the right combination of sensitivity, shock absorption, tip action and power for any crappie application," he claimed.

If you think crappie only bite tiny baits, check out this slab that Pickwick Lake, Alabama angler Brad Whitehead caught on a crankbait.

"Crappie Only Bite Tiny Baits"

"You ought to check out the shocked expressions on the faces of my crappie customers when they see the minnows I fish with," Jim Duckworth claimed. "They're used to fishing tiny tuffy minnows; I use 2- to 3-inch shiners, which are huge by comparison. My grandaddy caught his own bait when I was a kid, and he always fished with the biggest baits he could get and caught the biggest fish of anybody in town, so I reckon it's just in my blood."

Duckworth believes the biggest crappie aren't eating machines as many fishermen believe, but rather are highly selective about their groceries. "They feed less often than average-sized crappie, but prey on much larger minnows. I believe this gives them an advantage over lesser-sized fish, especially in murky water: when visibility is limited, tiny minnows tend to disappear, but a big one still puts out plenty of flash. A trophy-sized crappie can home in on a large minnow easily, regardless of water conditions."

Duckworth says the fact that a crappie will nail a bass crankbait further proves his point. "That's the equivalent of a human grabbing a whole cantaloupe in his mouth! One of my favorite post-spawn patterns is to troll quarter-ounce crankbaits at the edges of main-lake flats. Even lethargic suspended crappie will nail these without hesitation. If you're only catching small crappie, remember, size matters. Beef up your live bait or lure size and start tapping into a better class of fish."

"You Can't Catch Big-Crappie from Deep-Clear Lakes"

"Most anglers view classic crappie water as shallow, murky and full of brushy cover," Fred McClintock said. "Lowland reservoirs made fertile from agricultural run-off, such as Arkabutla and Enid lakes in Mississippi, have a reputation for producing giant crappie. By comparison, relatively few crappie fans have fished highland reservoirs. These gin-clear lakes are 180 degrees different than lowland fisheries: deep, clear, rocky and infertile. But once you understand how crappie behave in them, you can experience unbelievable action and catch some huge fish."

Cavernous, crystalline reservoirs such as Dale Hollow and Center Hill (both in Tennessee) are steadily gaining notoriety for producing monster slabs. McClintock has found these reservoirs' crappie fishing to be nothing short of extraordinary, but requiring an extraordinarily different approach than most crappie anglers are accustomed to. "It's more like striper fishing than crappie fishing — there's very little wood cover in the lake, and the crappie relate mainly to baitfish schools in open water," McClintock noted.

The most productive approach on a highland reservoir is slow-trolling jigs on long lines around shad schools, Fred has found. He varies jig weight, lure color and line length until he comes up with the right combination that gets into the fish zone and entices wary crappie to bite. His biggest fish so far: a whopping 3 3/4 pounds. "Highland reservoirs prove that there's more than one way to skin a cat — or a crappie," he concluded.

"Crappie Won't Bite in Frigid Water"

"Sun Belt anglers are responsible for this myth," Harold Morgan figures. "Most of them fish for crappie only in spring, and can't imagine sitting in a boat and dunking minnows on days cooler than 65 degrees. But as Northern anglers know, crappie can bite aggressively in cold water — even through the ice."

Morgan recalled a guide trip on Priest Reservoir near Nashville last February. "It was 18 degrees that morning and we broke ice launching the boat. We found fish holding tight to brushpiles in 17 feet of water along a creek channel dropoff; you had to lower a live minnow straight down into the brush to get bit. By noon, the fish had risen out of the cover and were suspending over it; we found that by dropping our baited rigs to the bottom and slowly reeling up through the school, we'd catch quality crappie consistently."

The best winter crappie bite tends to occur where some water movement is present, Morgan has discovered. "I've had my best luck from the upper end to about midway down a reservoir in winter, as opposed to in the lower end. There, current flow is stronger, the water more highly oxygenated, baitfish more concentrated and crappie more abundant."

SECRETS OF AMERICA'S TOP CRAPPIE GUIDES

Garry with another big 'un!

Attaboy Harold!

PHOTO ALBUM

Waitin' for the bobber to go down...

Jim with his homemade PVC "brushpiles"

SECRETS OF AMERICA'S TOP CRAPPIE GUIDES

Jim with a Kentucky Lake Toad

Some serious sinkers!

PHOTO ALBUM

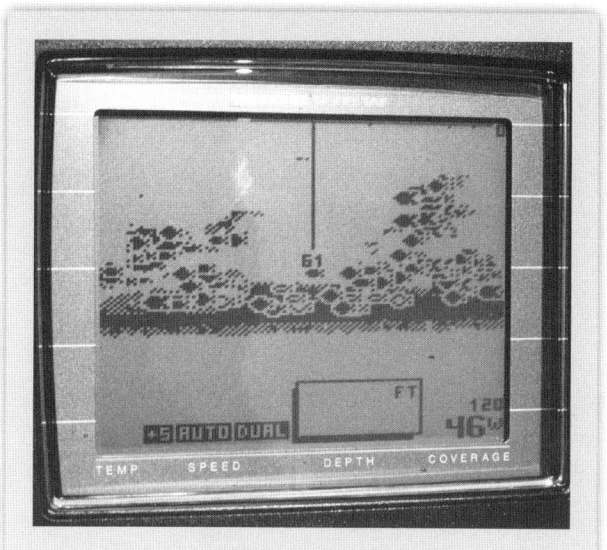

A huge school of slabs in deep water

Garry scores again!

SECRETS OF AMERICA'S TOP CRAPPIE GUIDES

Jim with two nice ones from Priest Lake

A big crankbait crappie

PHOTO ALBUM

Steve whacked 'em on Kentucky Lake!

Steve with Kentucky Lake's finest

SECRETS OF AMERICA'S TOP CRAPPIE GUIDES

Crappie WILL bite during a cold front!

Got poles?

PHOTO ALBUM

Jim doubles up

Kentucky Lake twins

Harold's custom minnow bucket

DON WIRTH

Don Wirth has been writing about freshwater fishing for nearly 40 years. His award-winning articles and photographs appear regularly in *Outdoor Life, Field & Stream, Bassmaster, North American Fisherman, Bassin', In-Fisherman* and *Crappie World*. Wirth's other books include *Bill Dance's Fishing Tips, Catch Bass With Doug Hannon* and *Smallmouth Guide*. He lives in Nashville, Tennessee.

My Favorite Fishing Spots

NOTES

BILL DANCE
"AMERICA'S FAVORITE FISHERMAN"

shares his greatest bass fishing tips with award-winning outdoor writer/photographer Don Wirth in this popular illustrated guide for novice or expert anglers everywhere.

BILL DANCE'S FISHING TIPS

"AMERICA'S FAVORITE FISHERMAN" REVEALS HIS SECRETS FOR CATCHING BASS, CRAPPIE, WALLEYE & MORE!

by Bill Dance with Don Wirth

Only $6.99 plus $3.00 shipping.

To Order Call 1-800-891-7323

Available from The Publisher

Secrets of America's Top Crappie Guides @ $14.99 + $3.00 S&H
Bill Dance's Fishing Tips @ $6.99 + $3.00 S&H
or
Both titles @ $17.95 + $5.00 S&H a 20% savings!

Great Gift! Great Reading!

VISA, MasterCard, American Express, Discover accepted
All orders shipped day of receipt.

For other titles go to www.premiumpressamerica.com